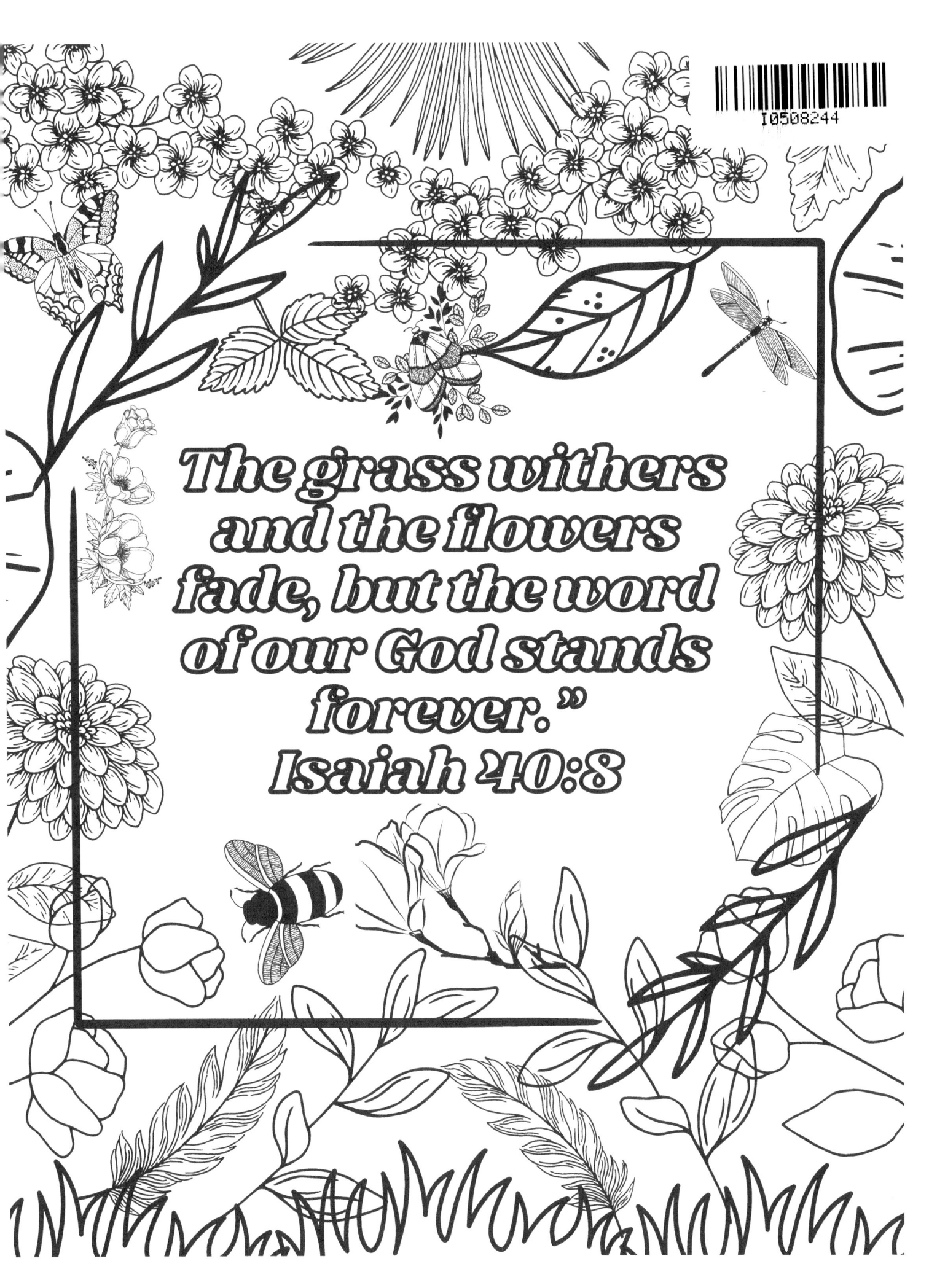

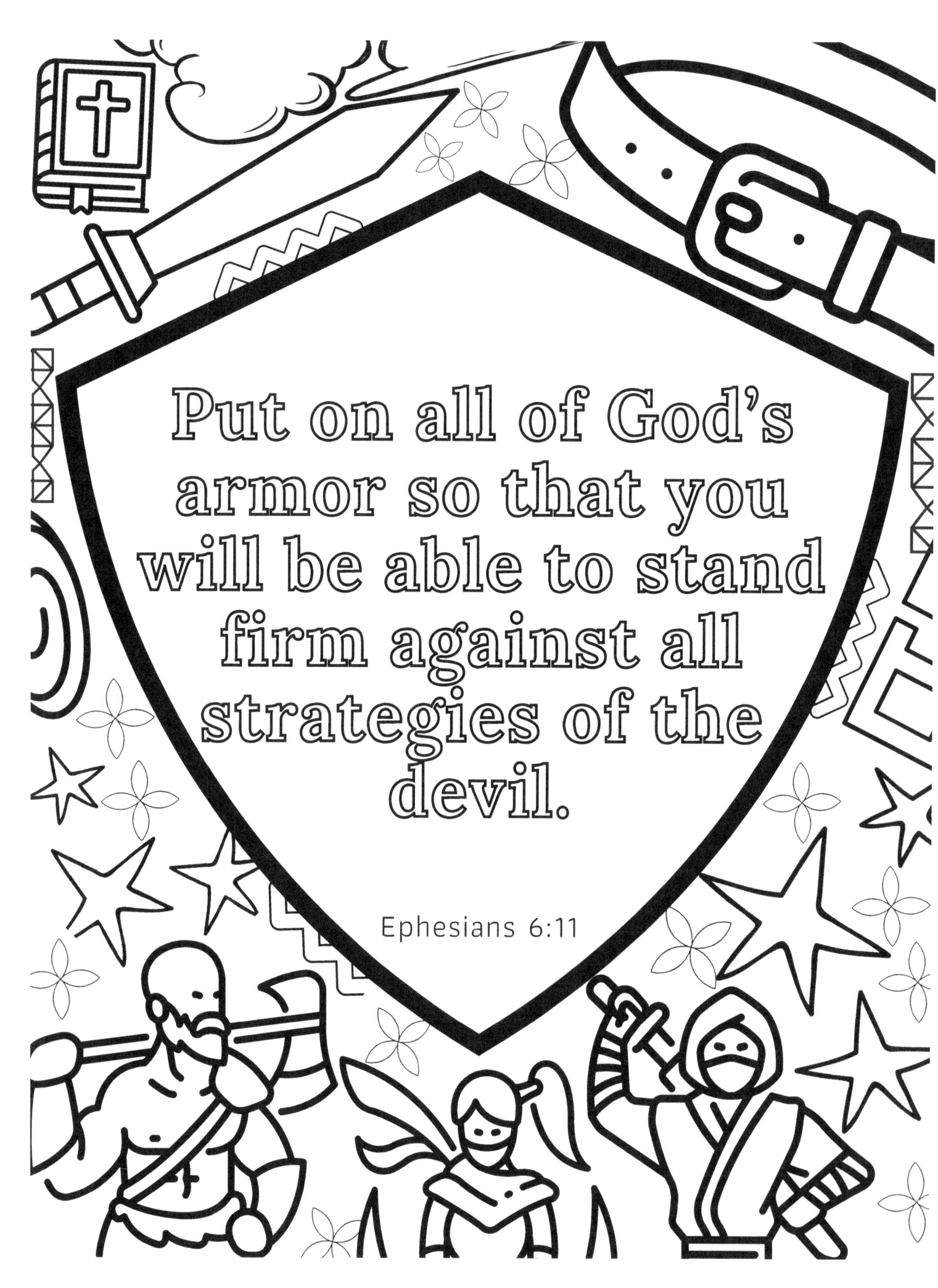

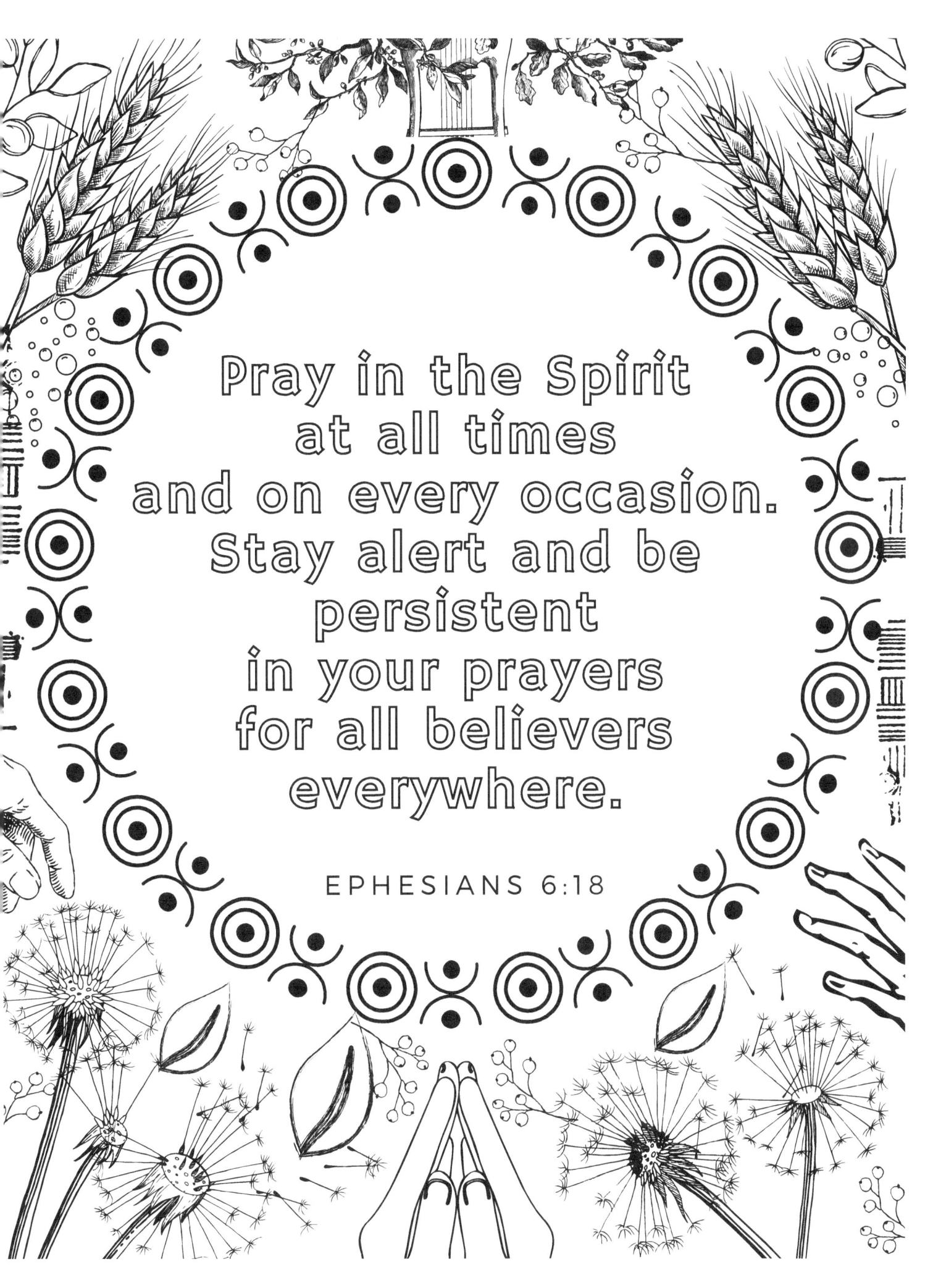

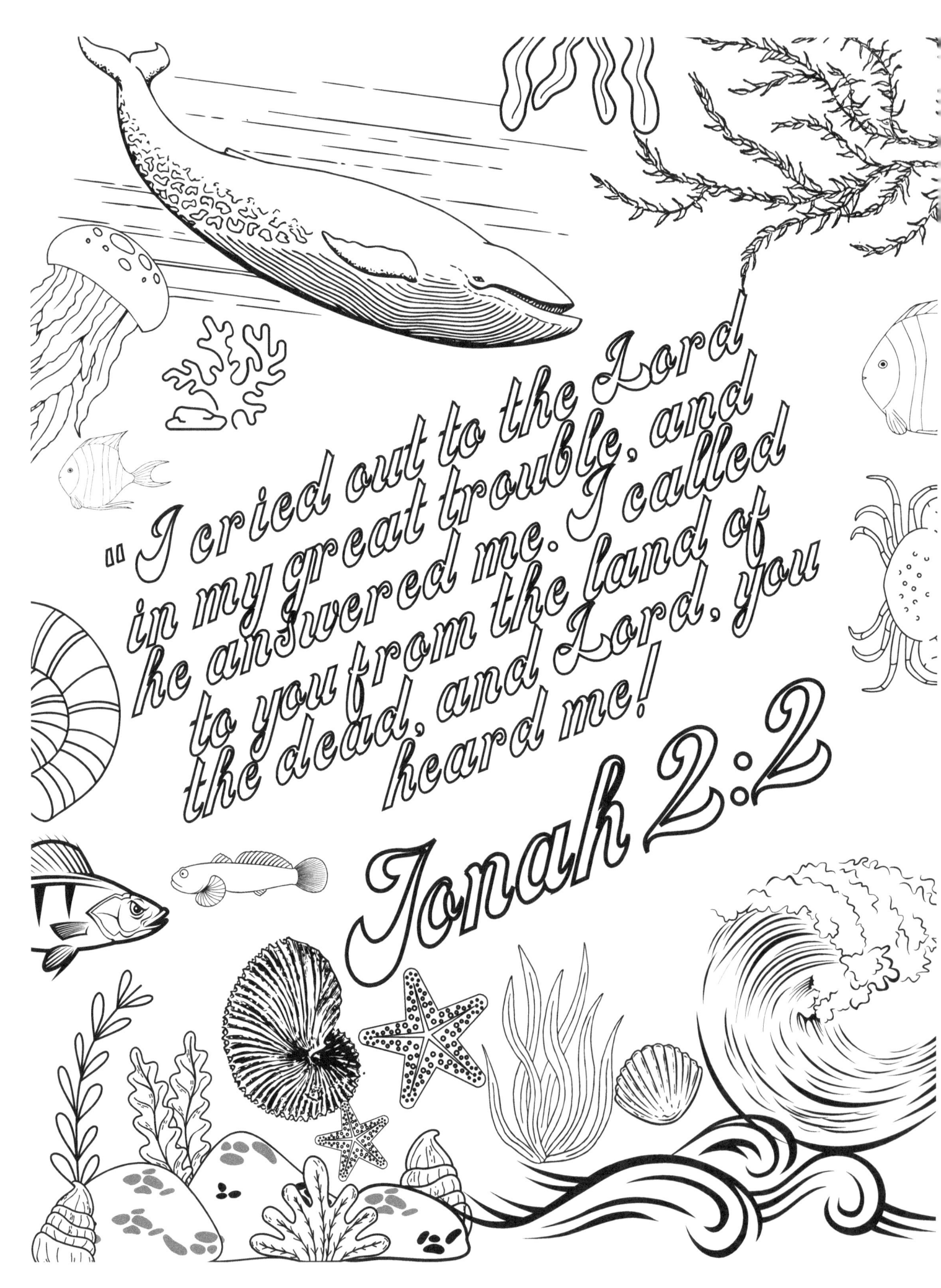

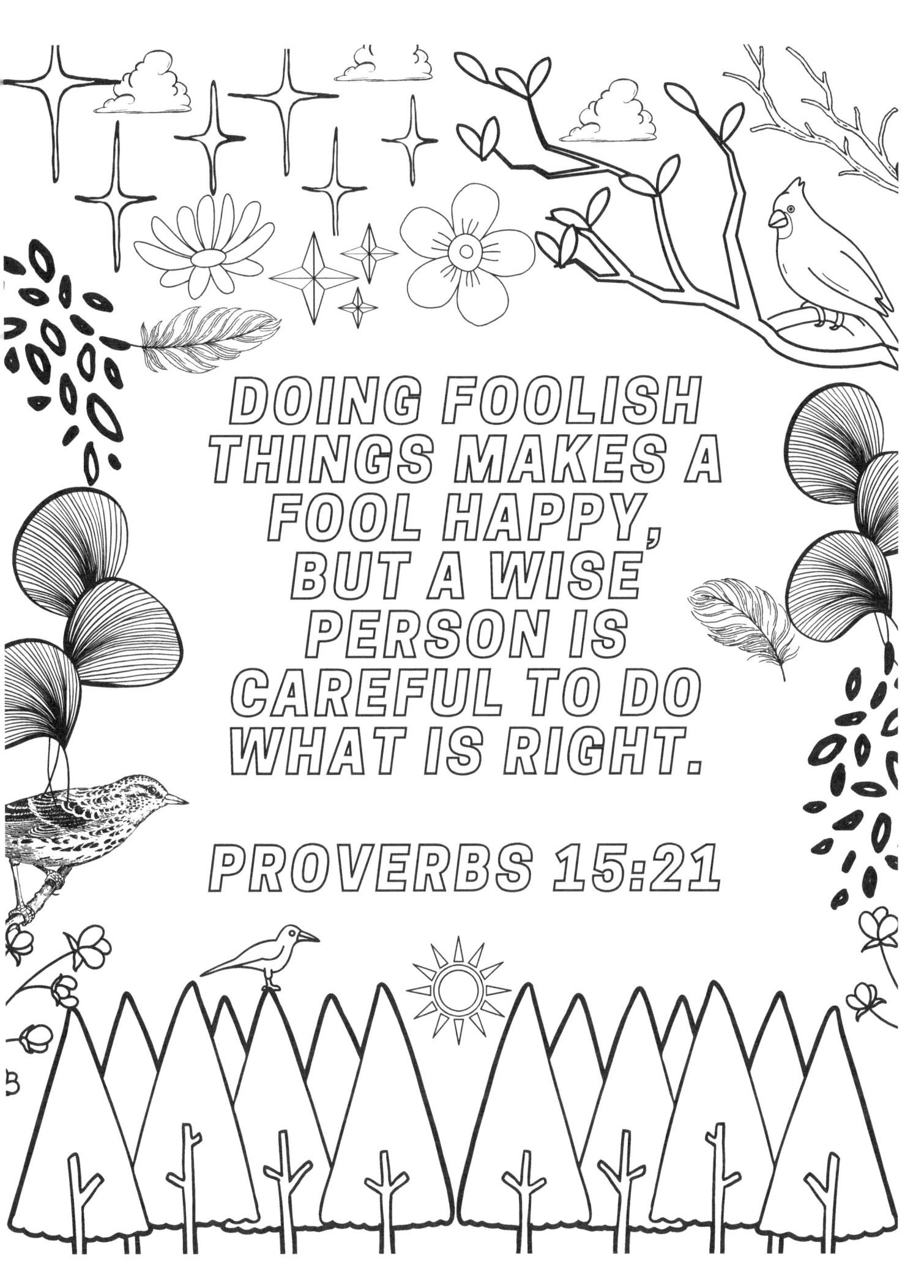

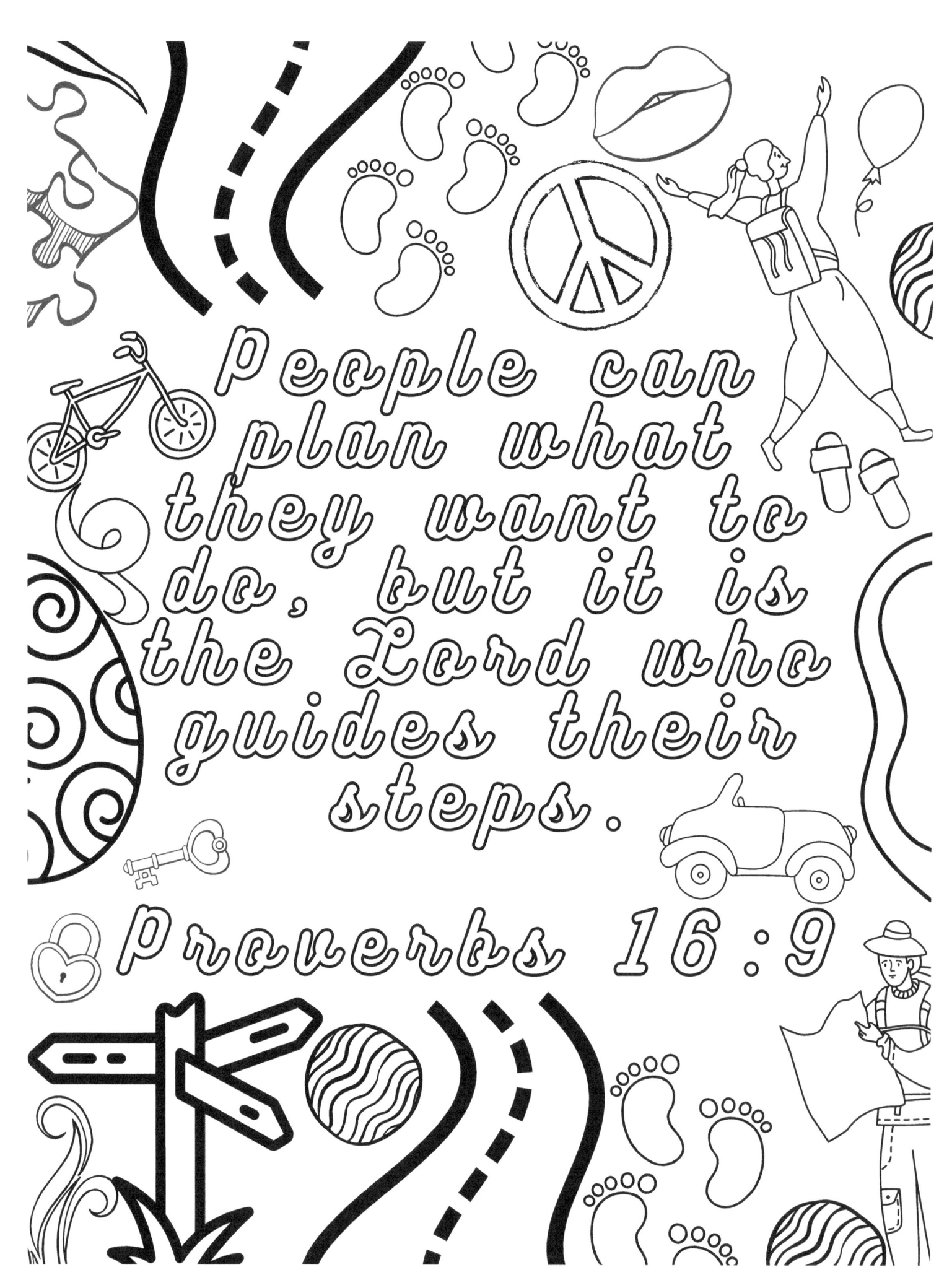

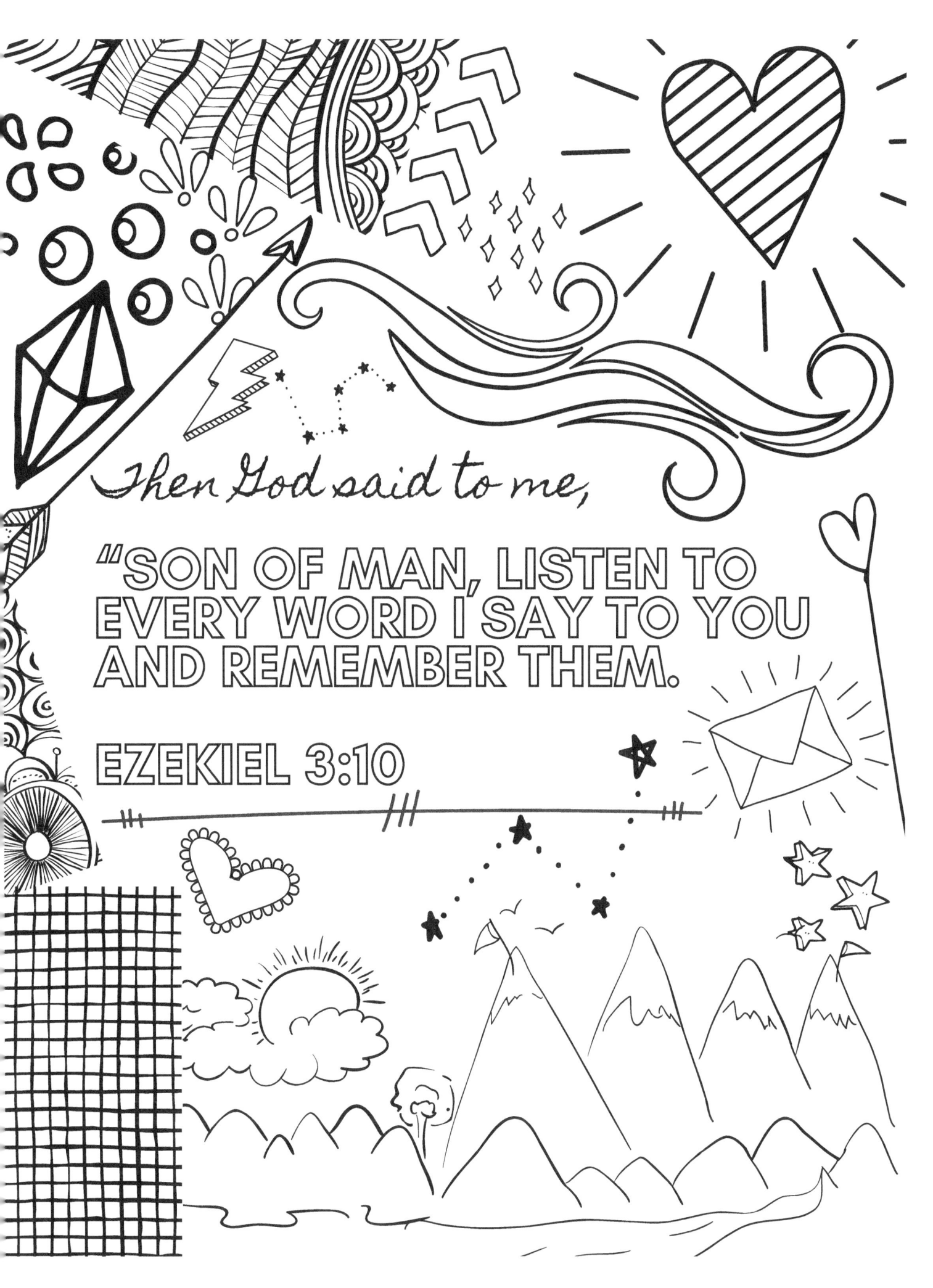

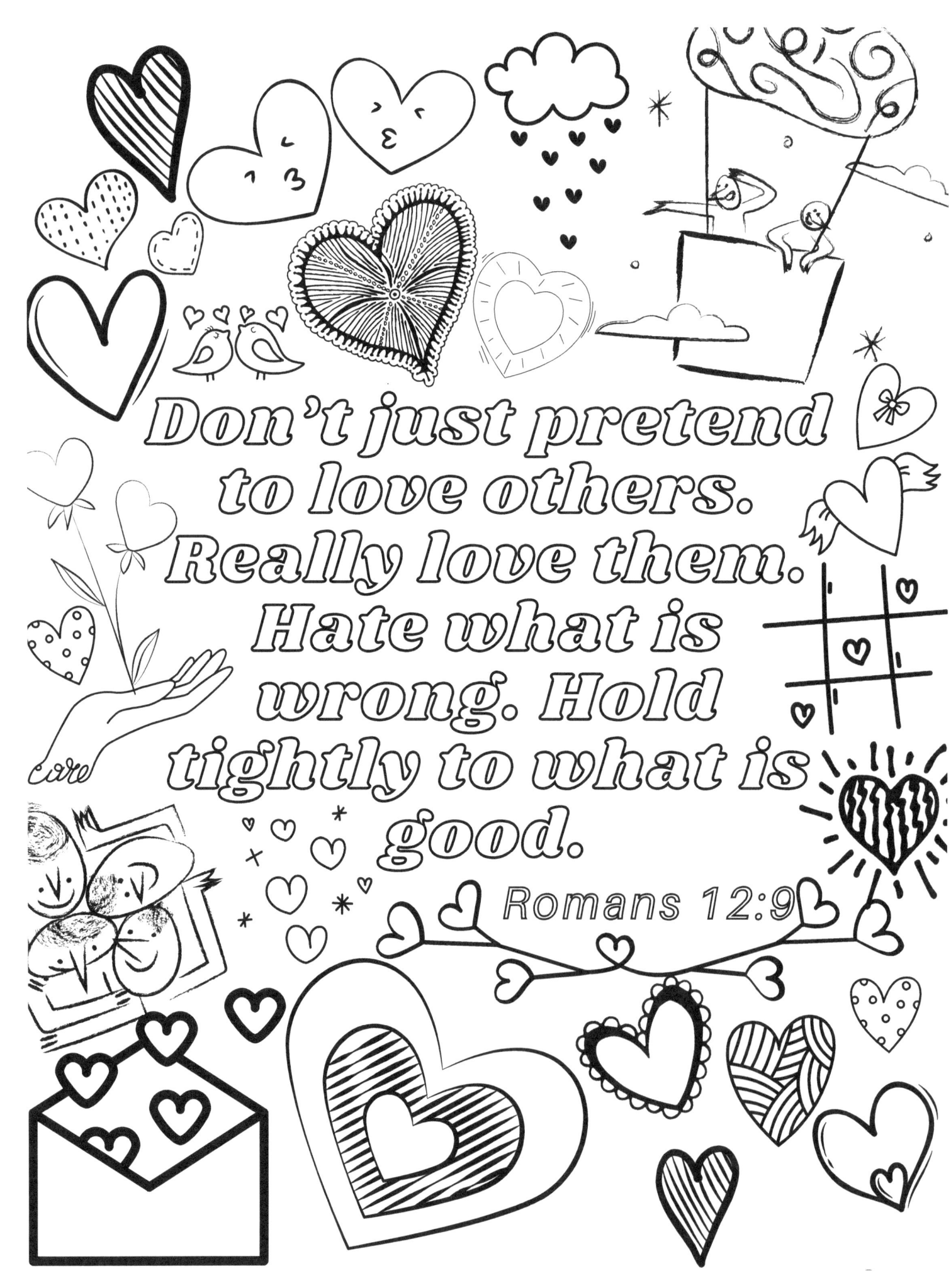

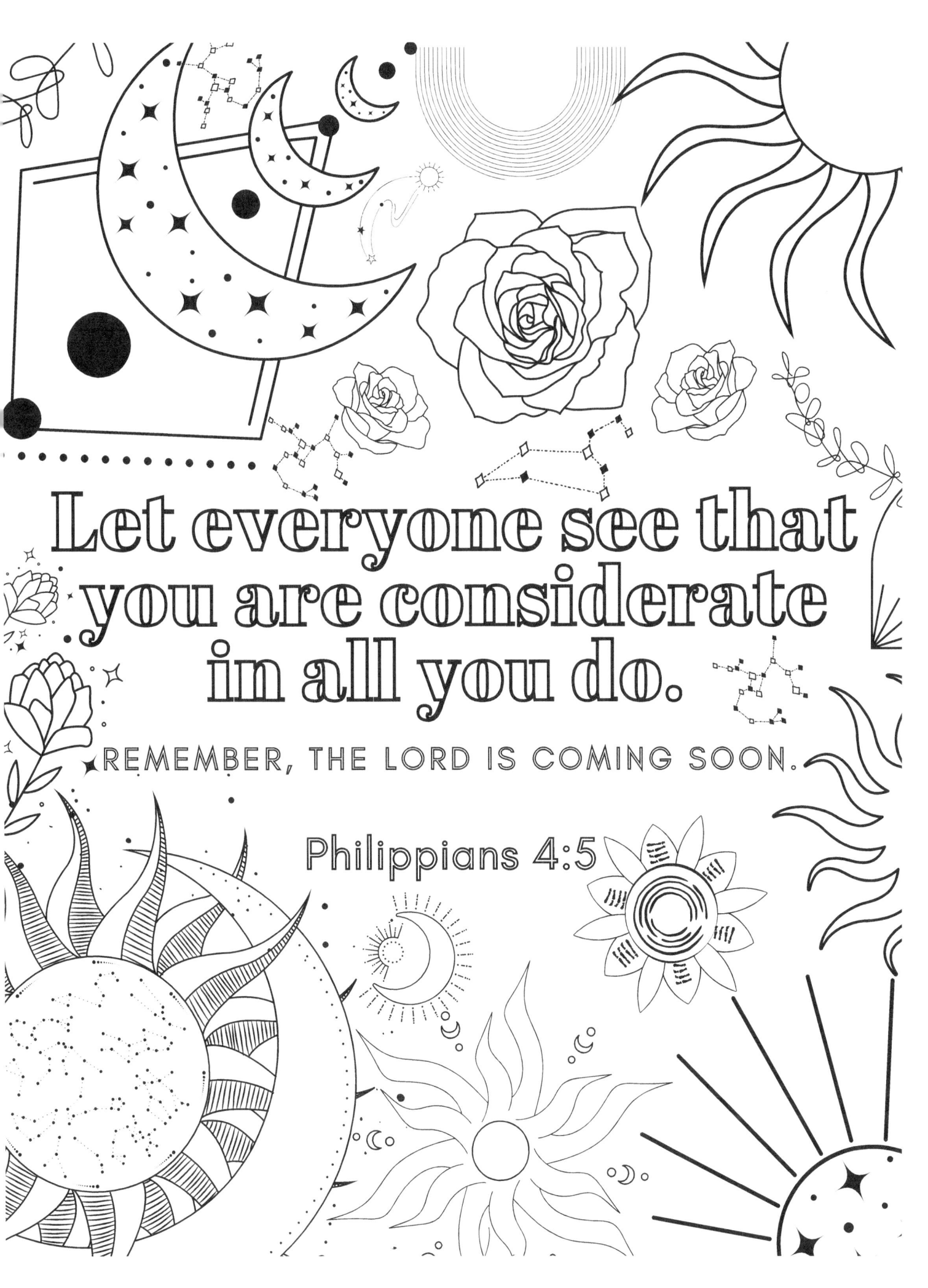

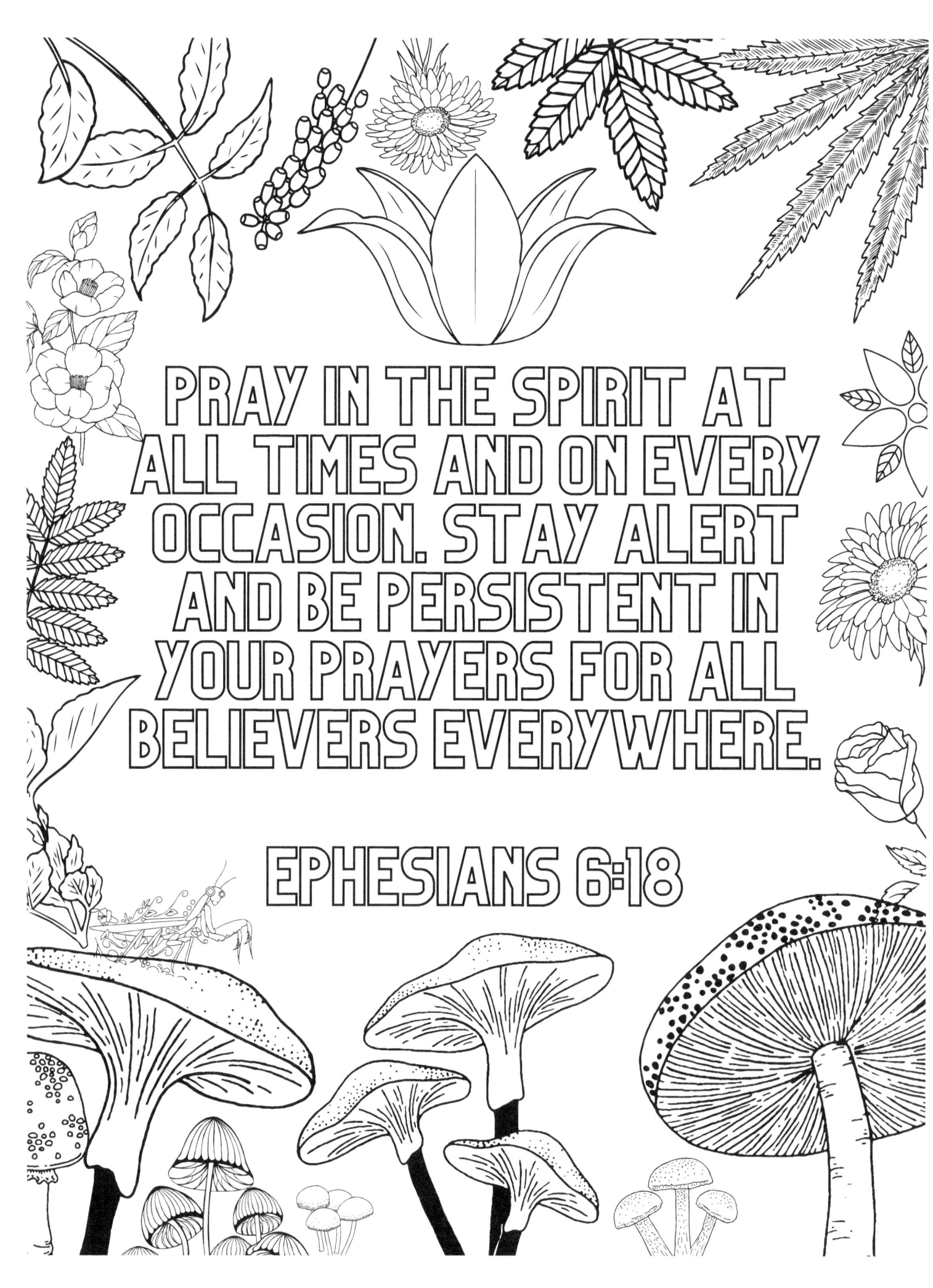

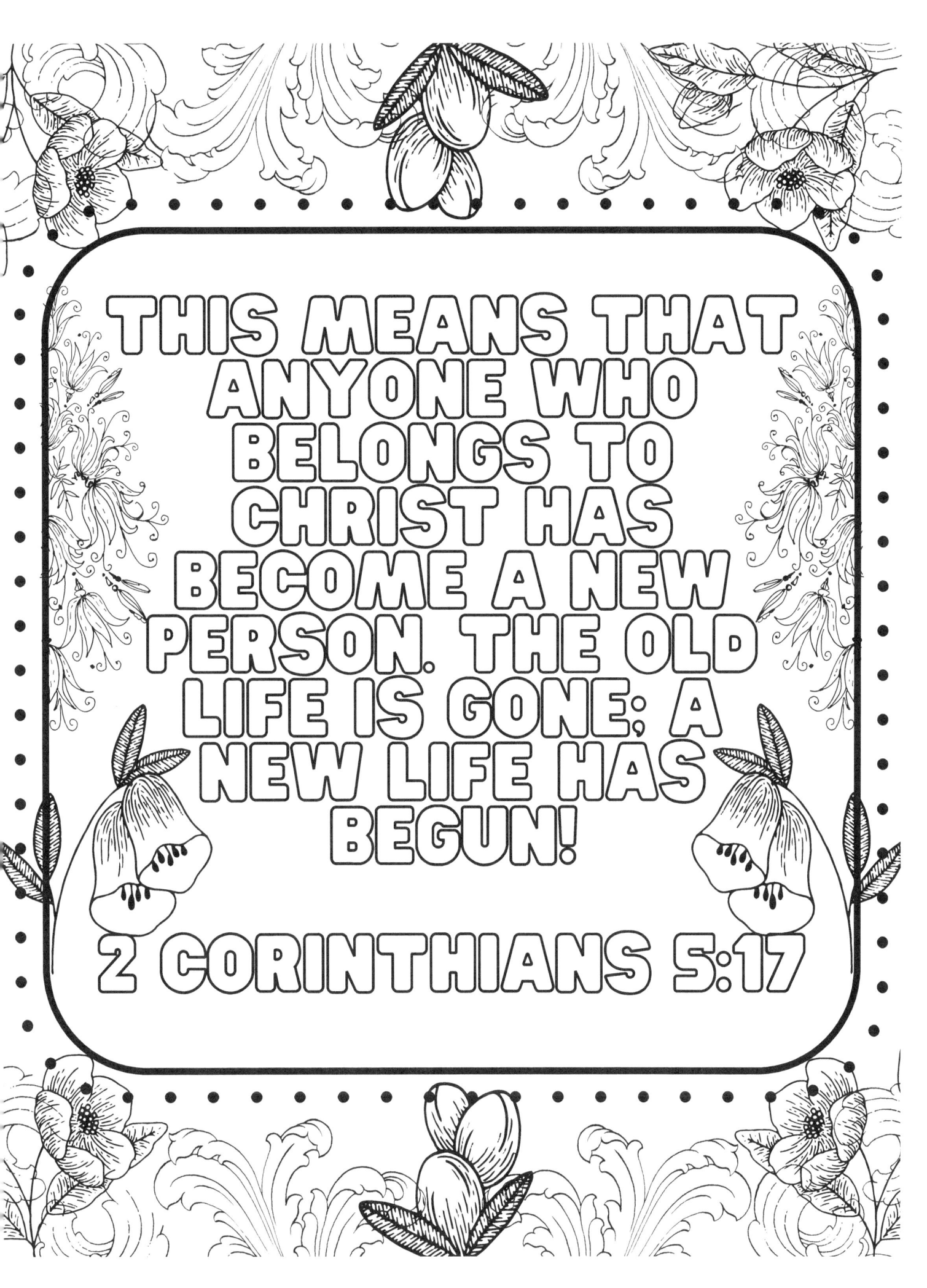

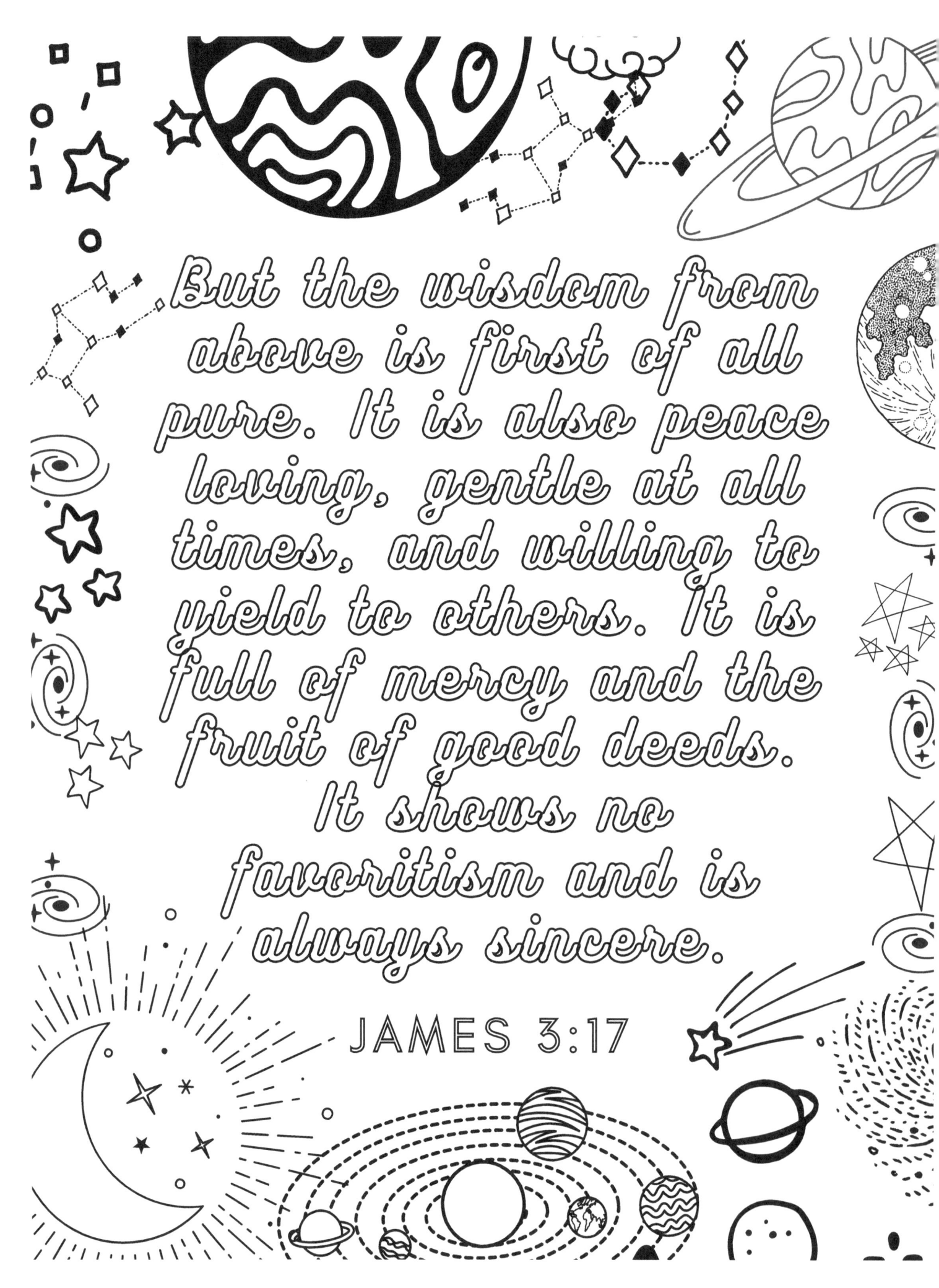

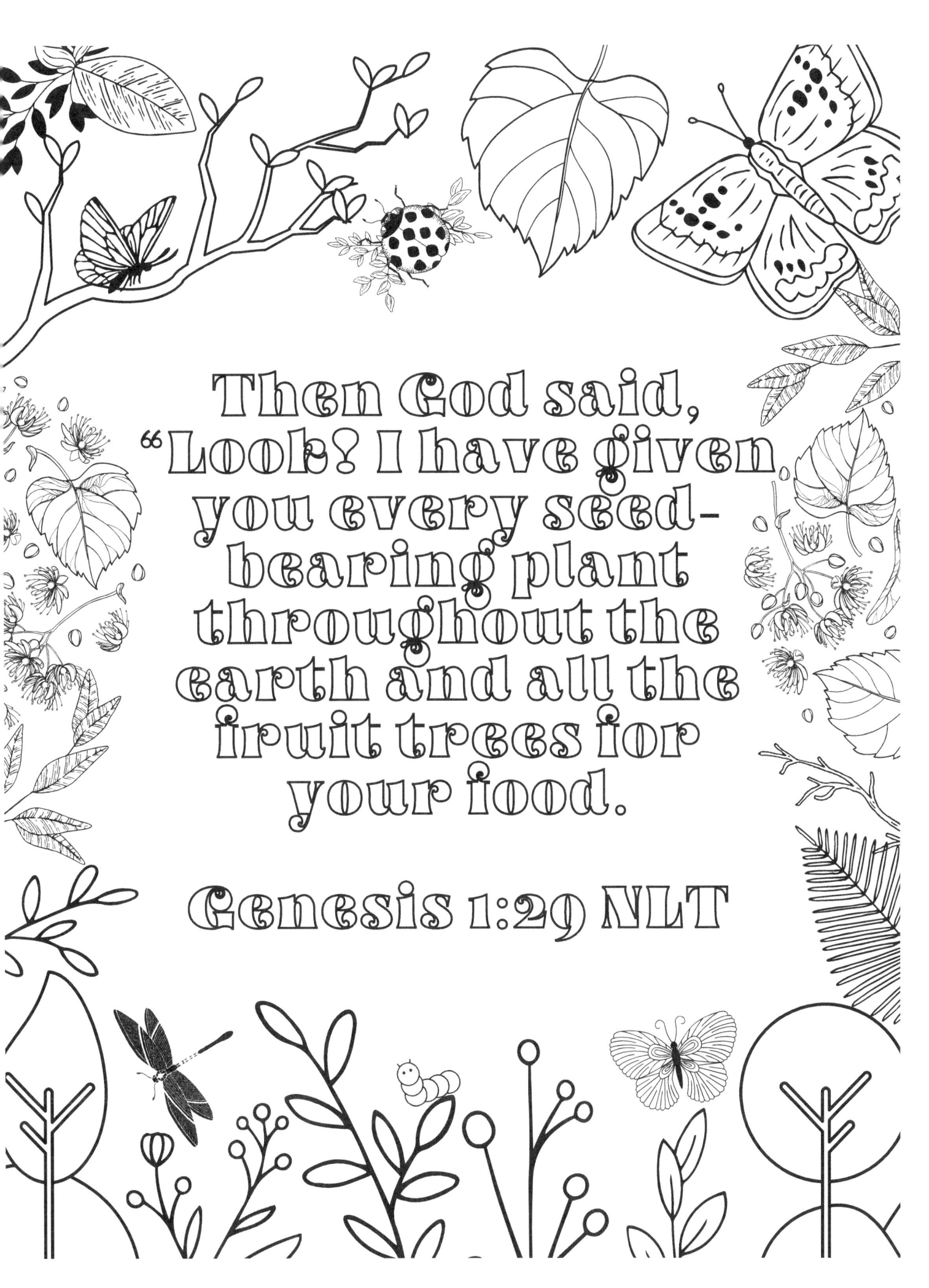

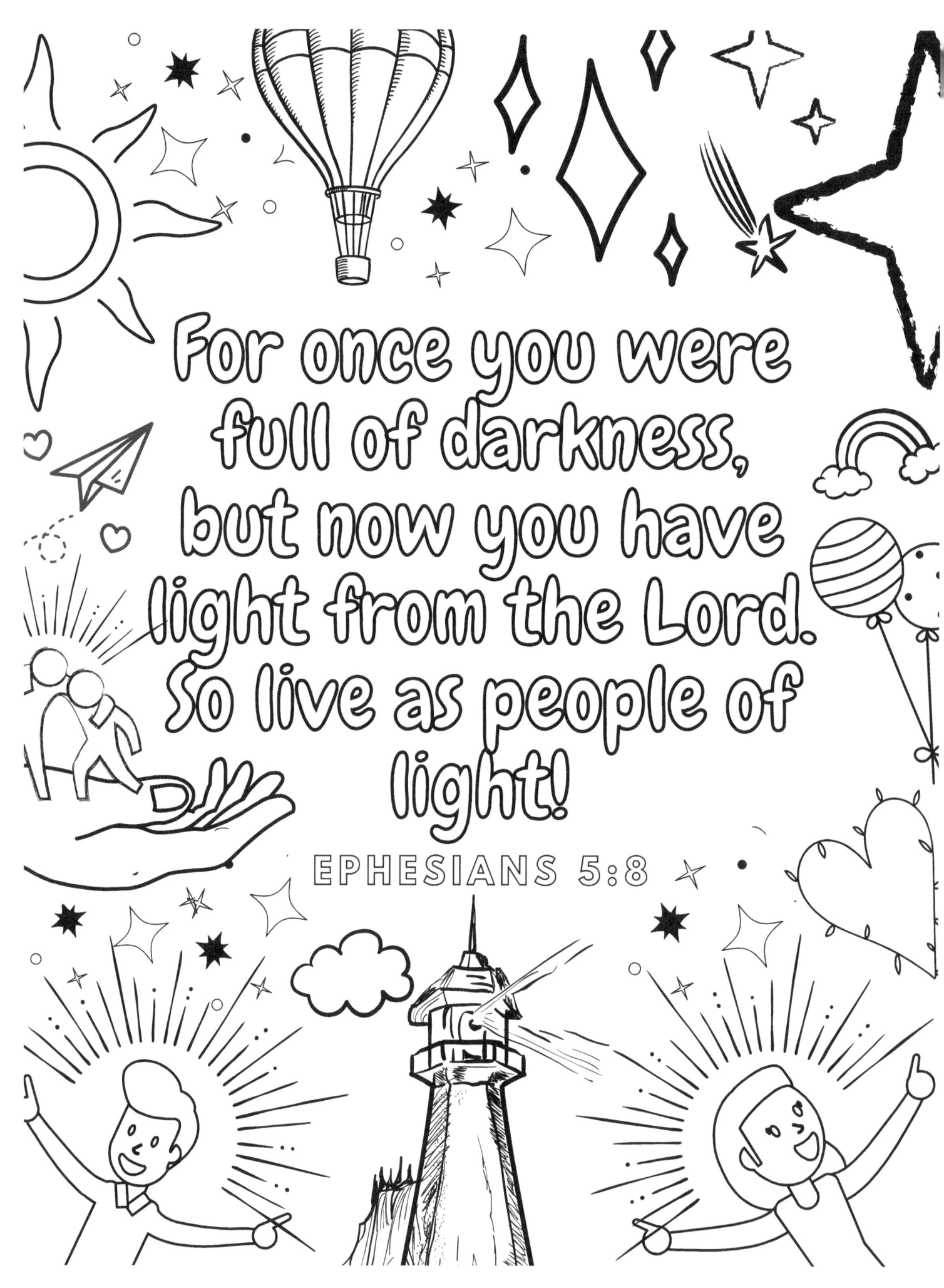

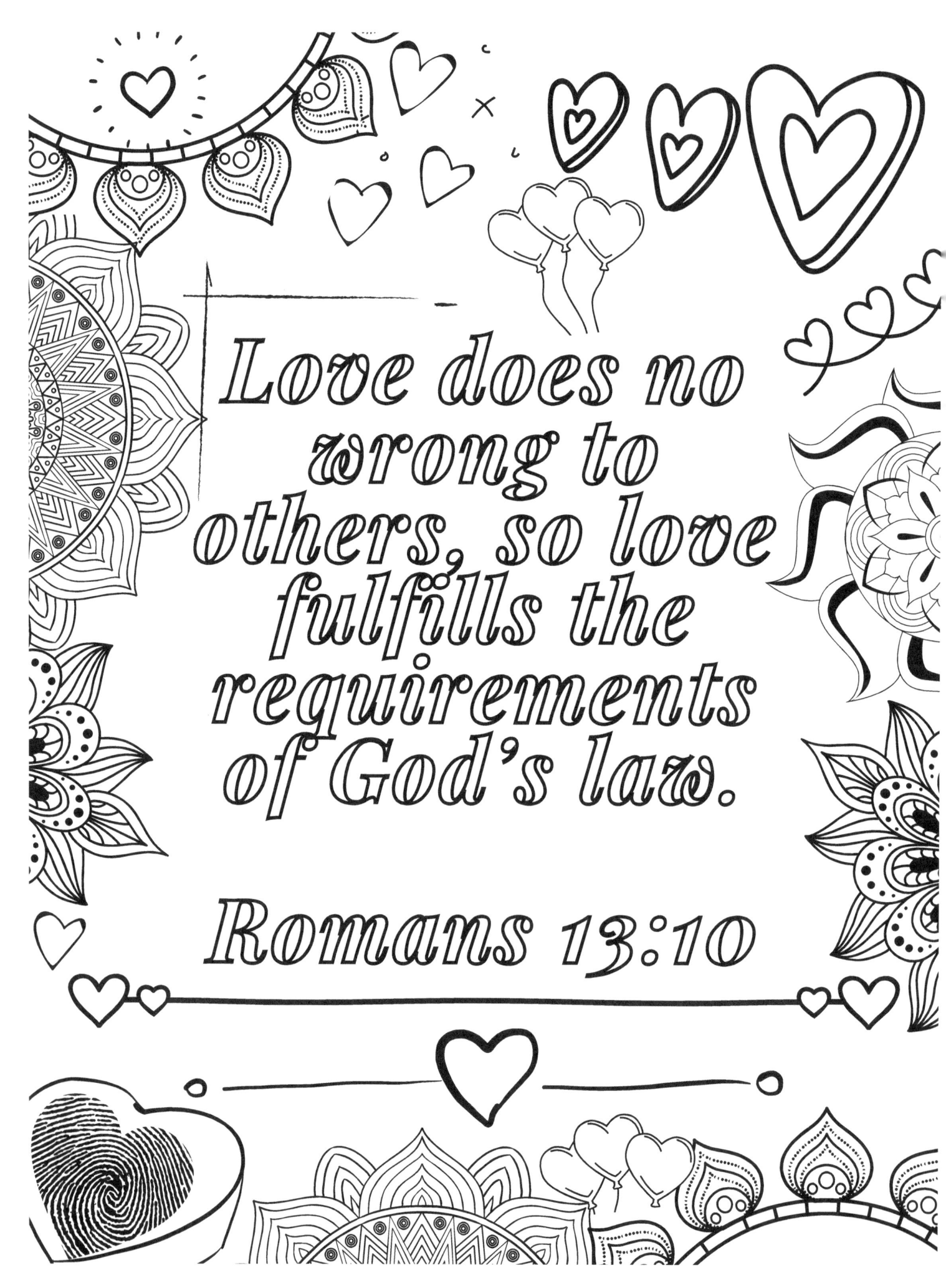

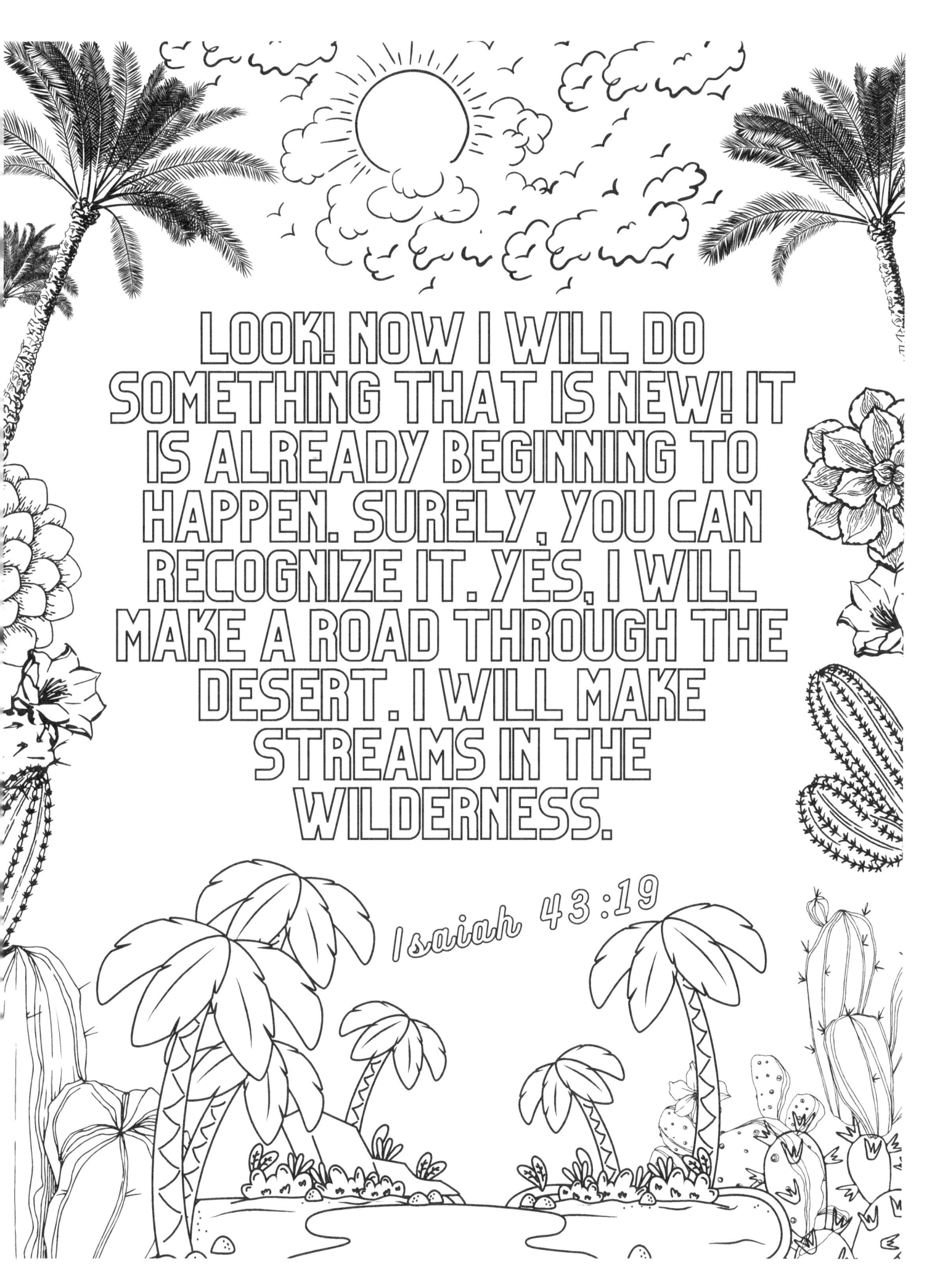

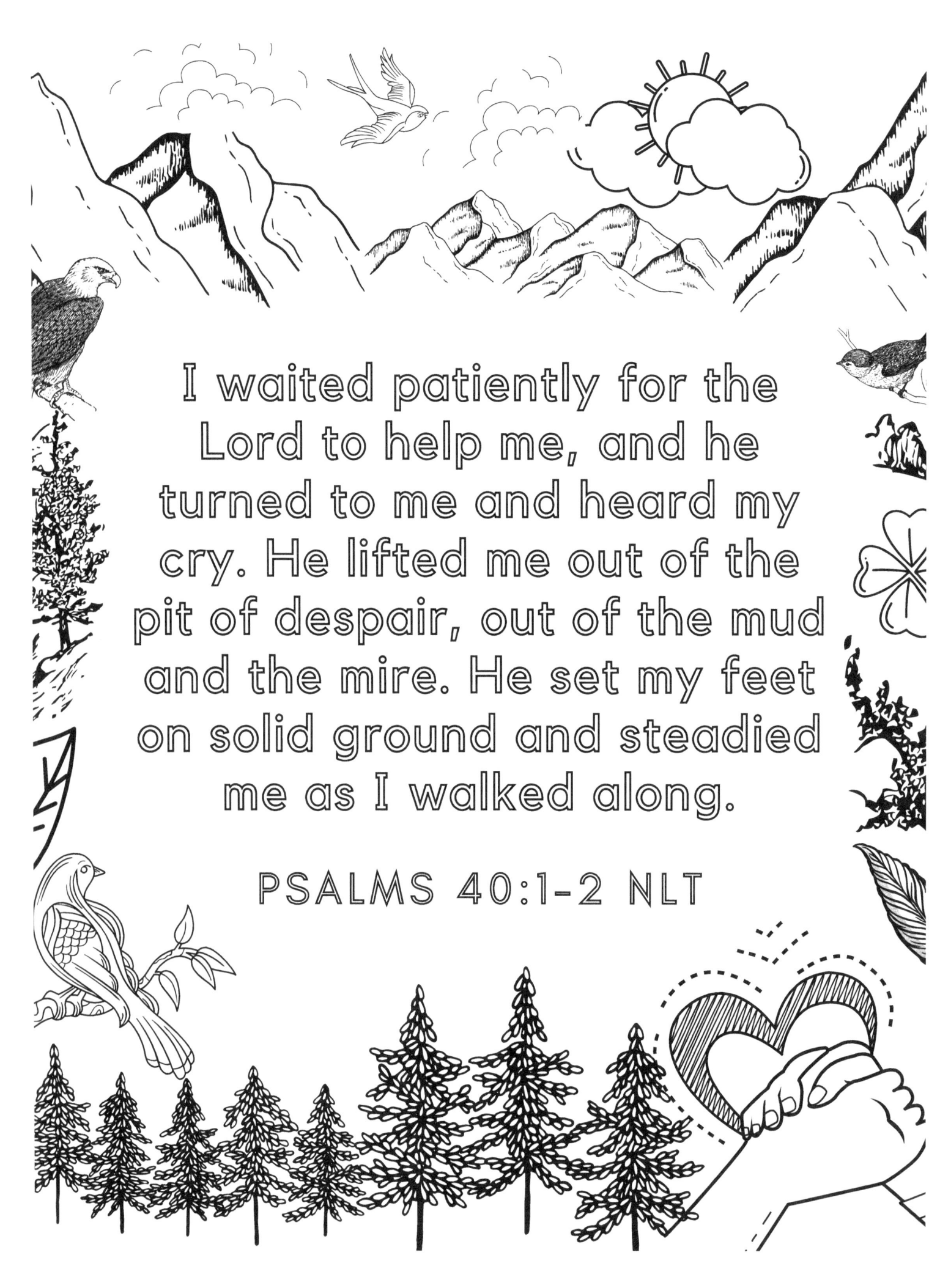

I waited patiently for the Lord to help me, and he turned to me and heard my cry. He lifted me out of the pit of despair, out of the mud and the mire. He set my feet on solid ground and steadied me as I walked along.

PSALMS 40:1-2 NLT

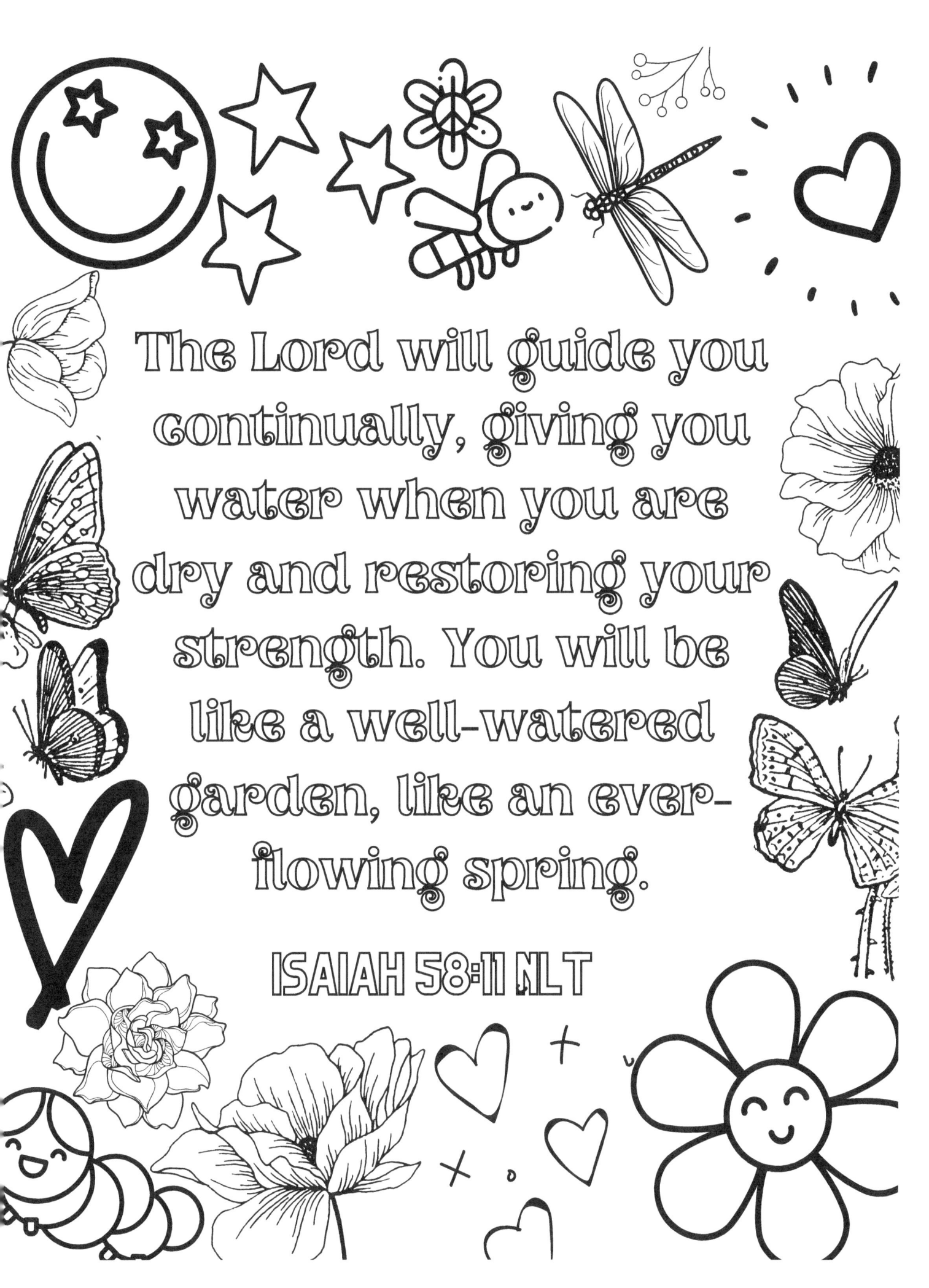

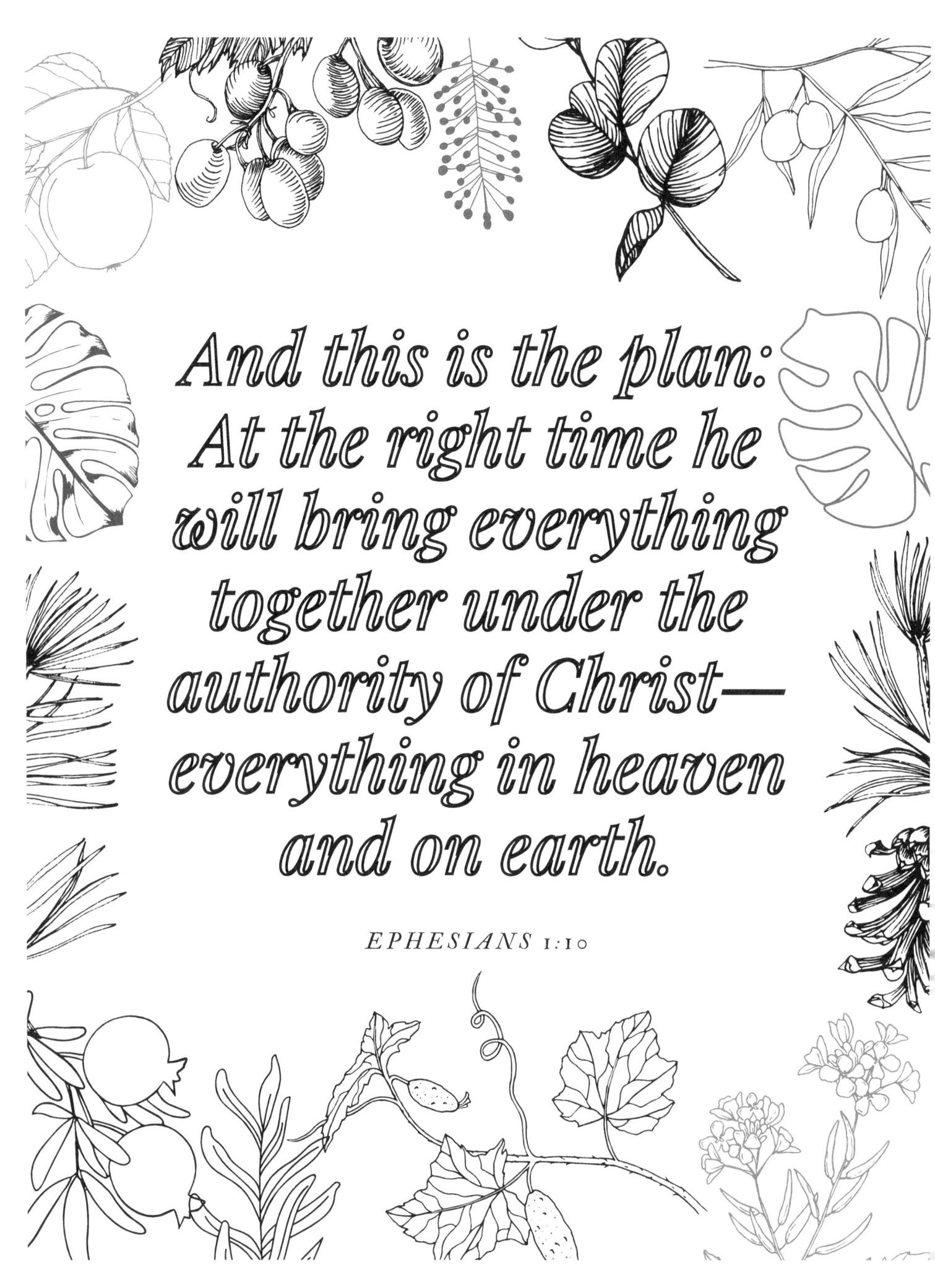

And this is the plan: At the right time he will bring everything together under the authority of Christ— everything in heaven and on earth.

EPHESIANS 1:10

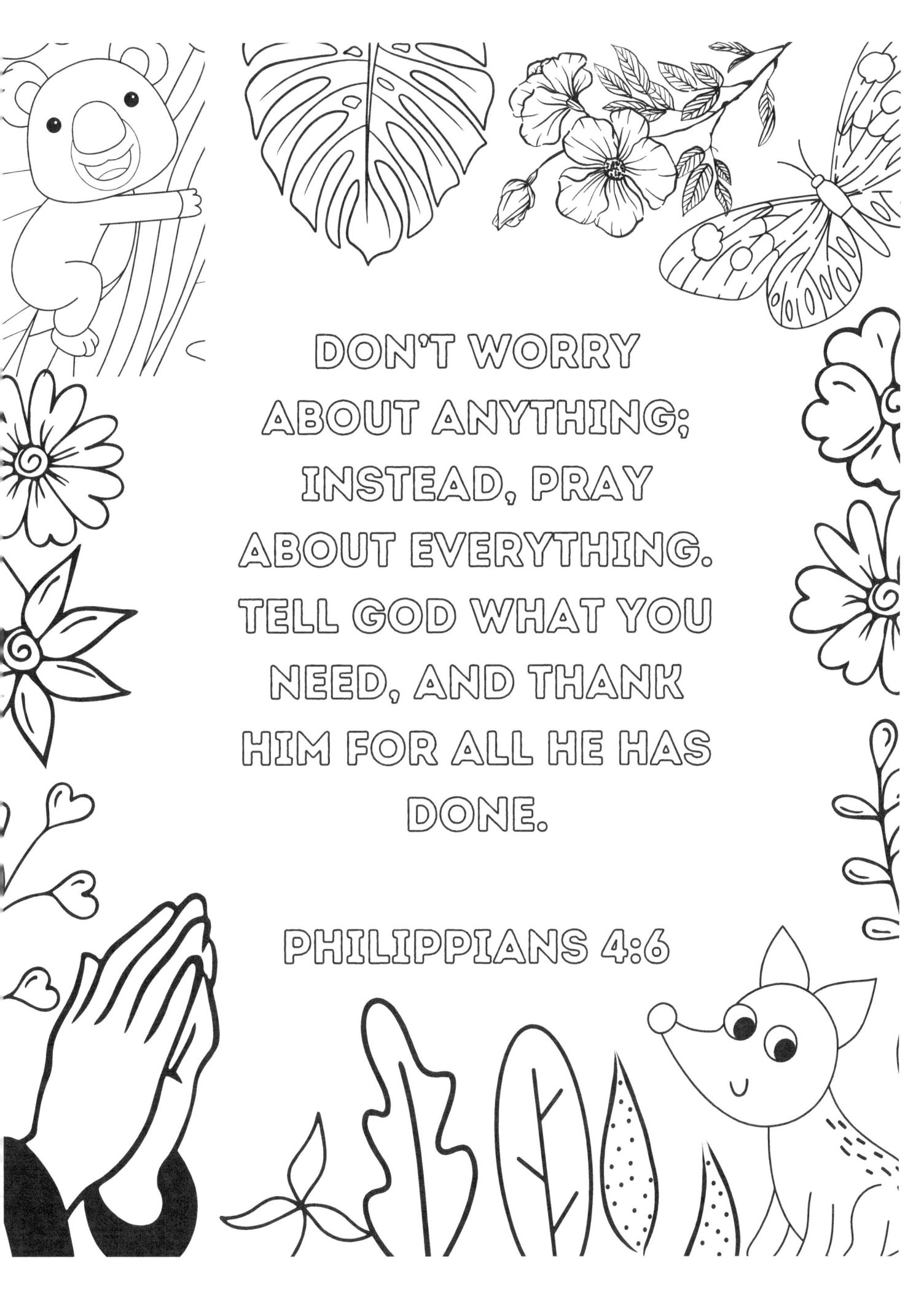

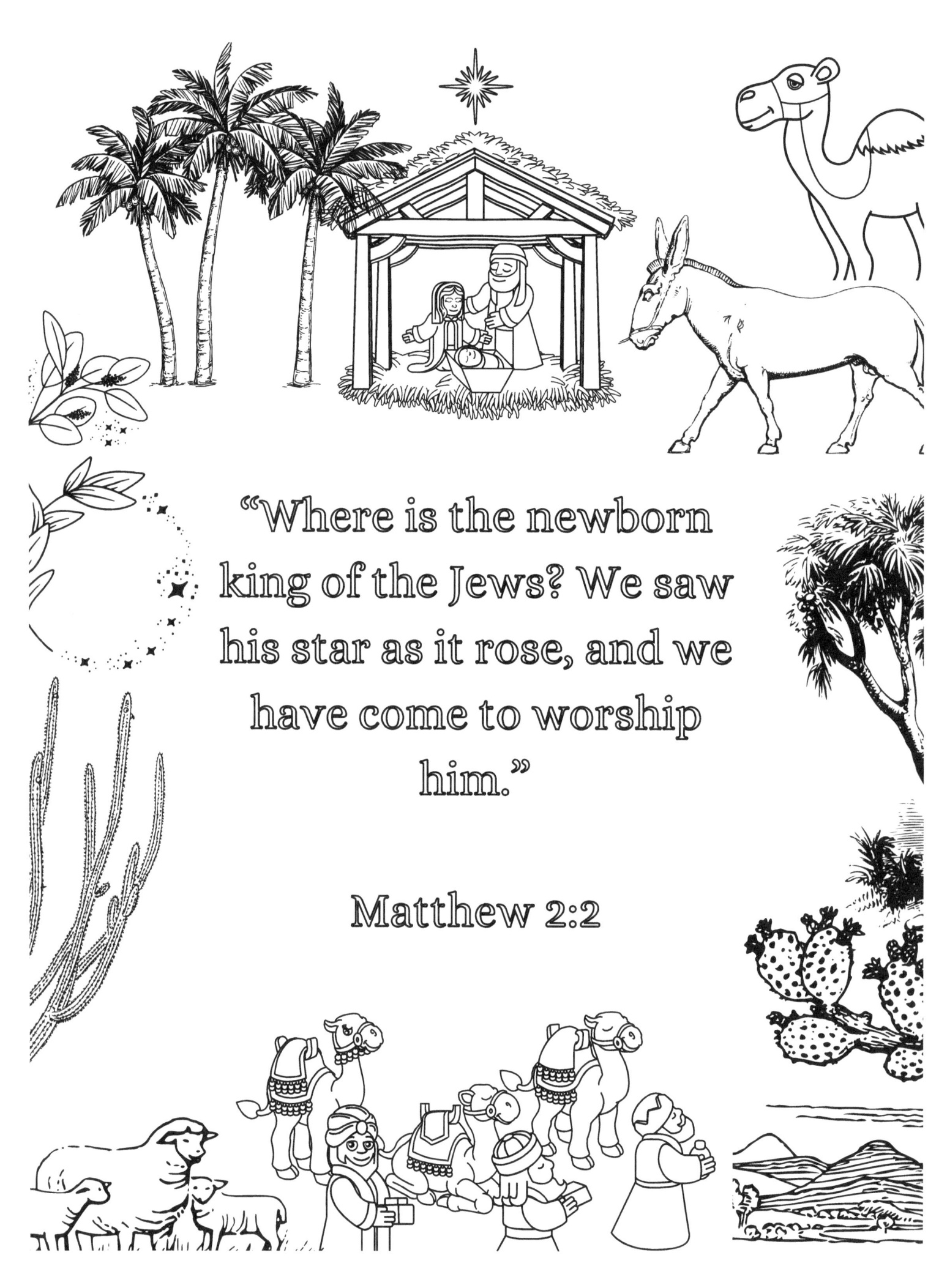

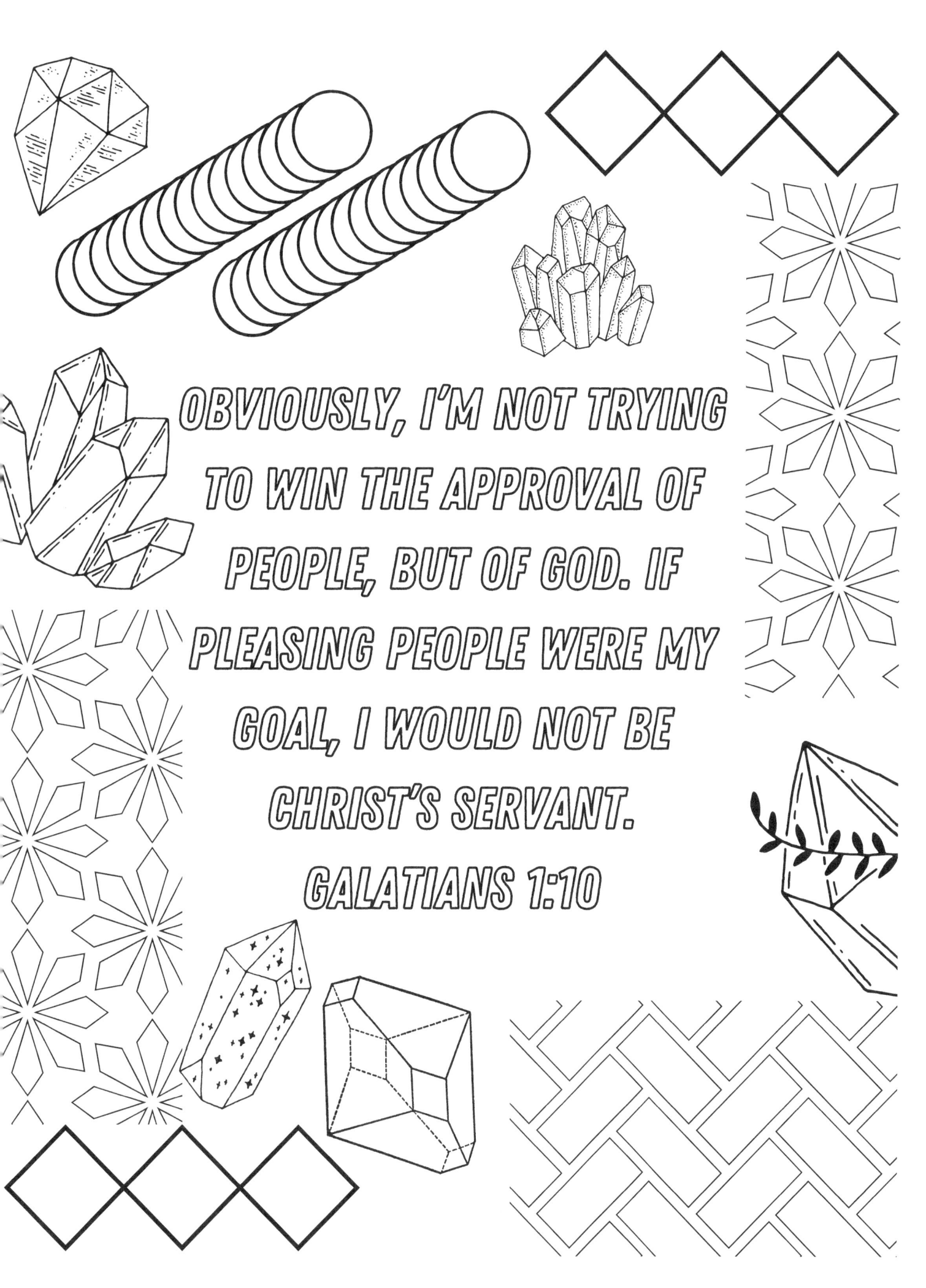

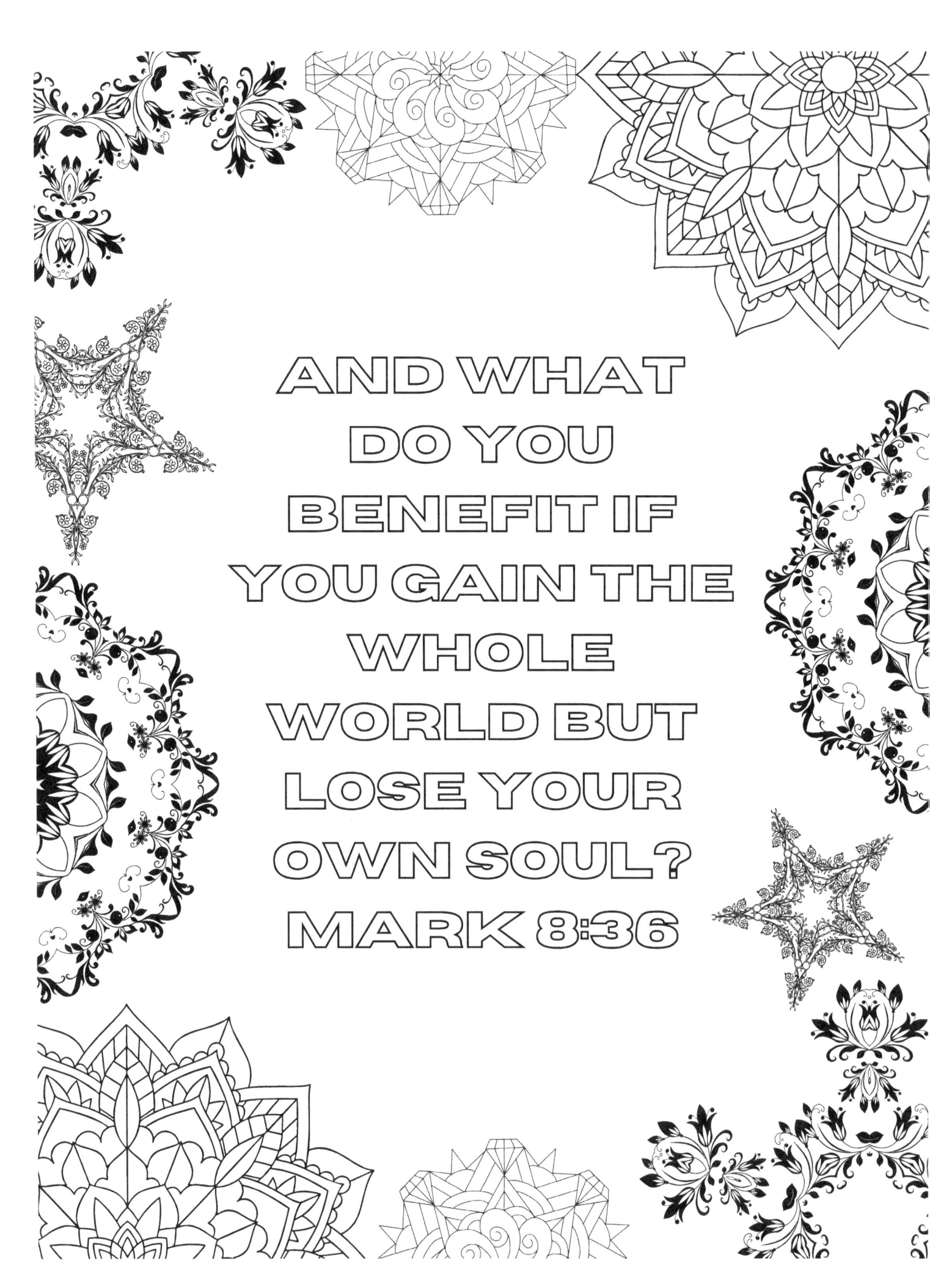

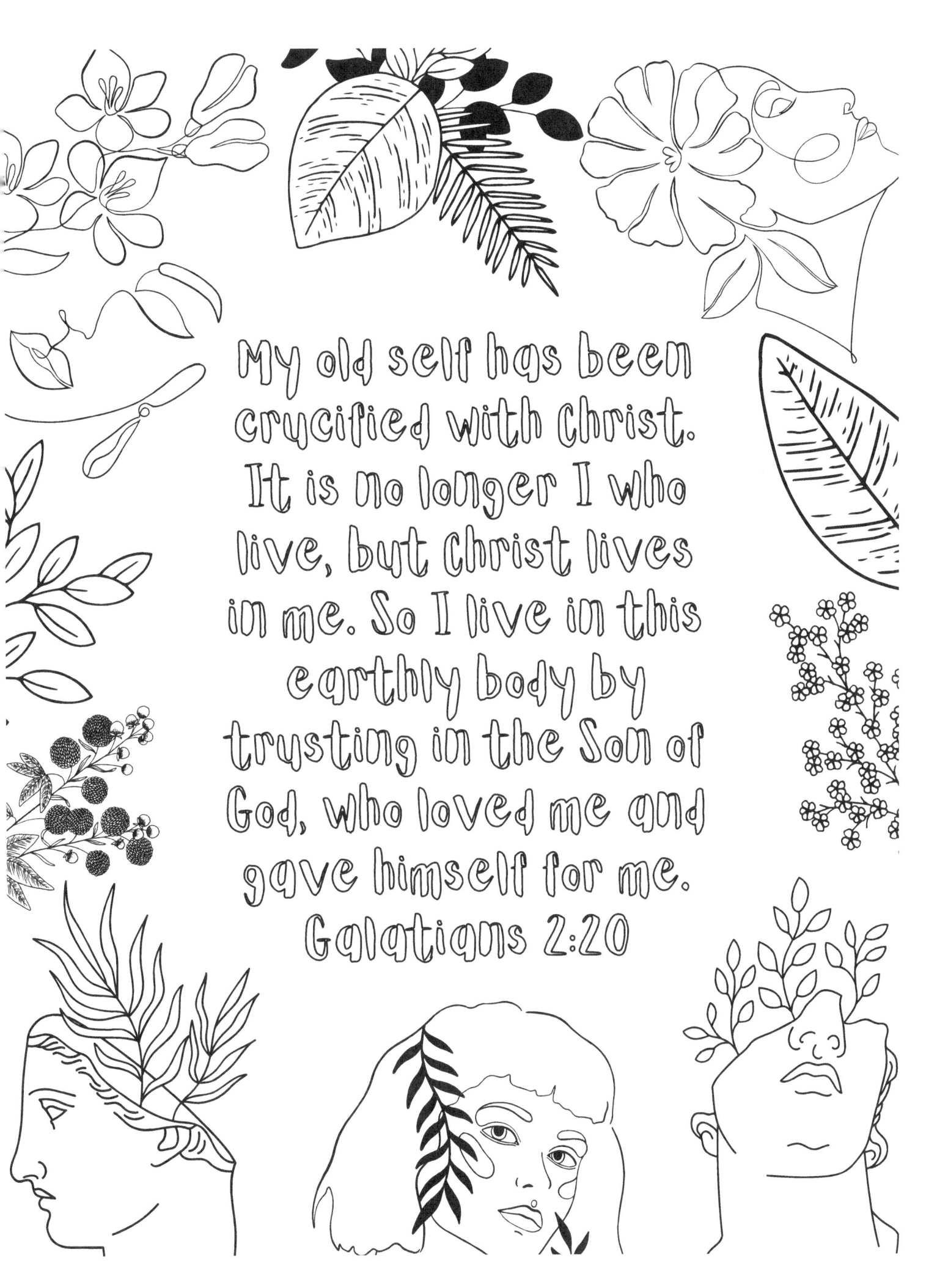

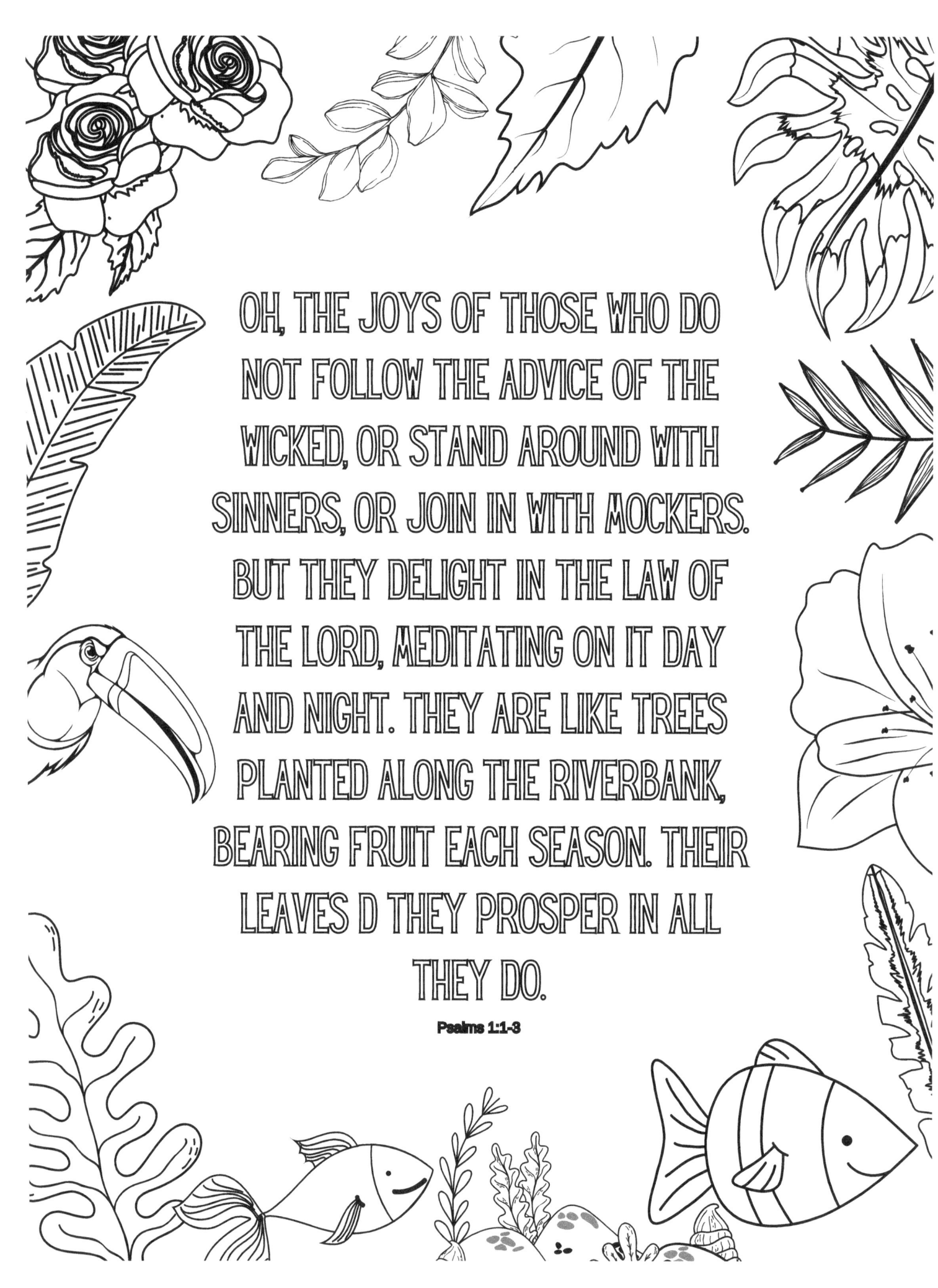

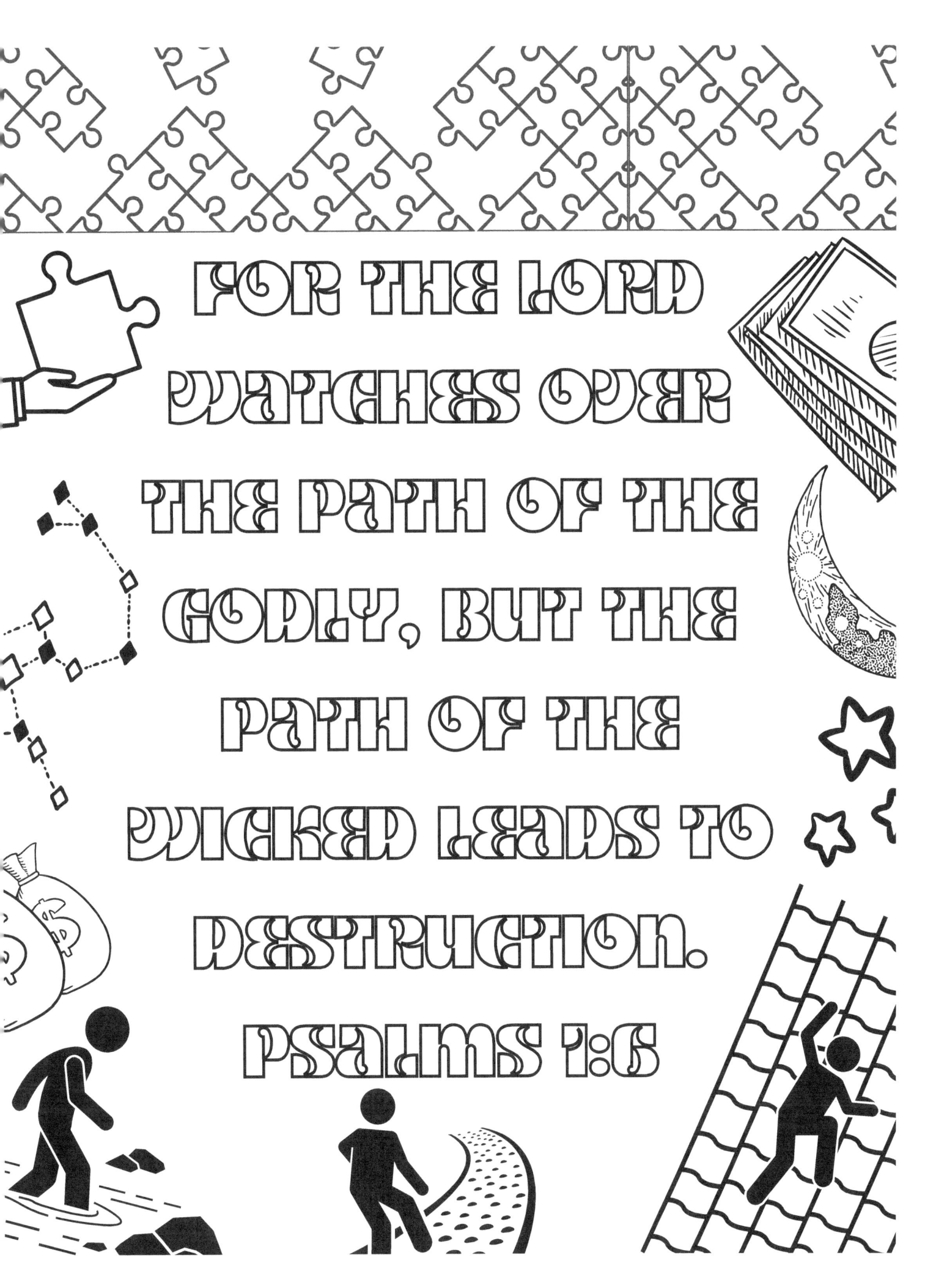

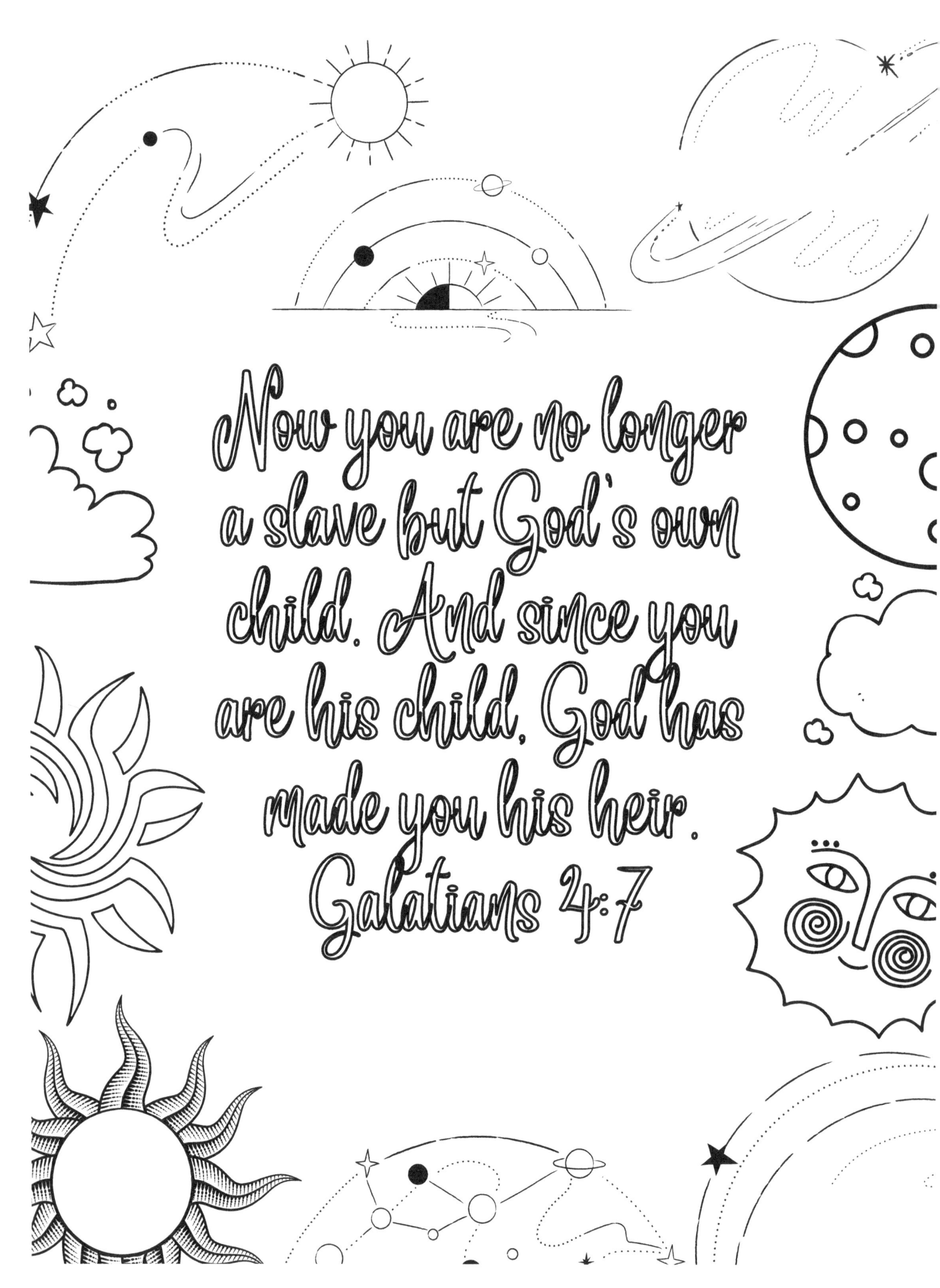

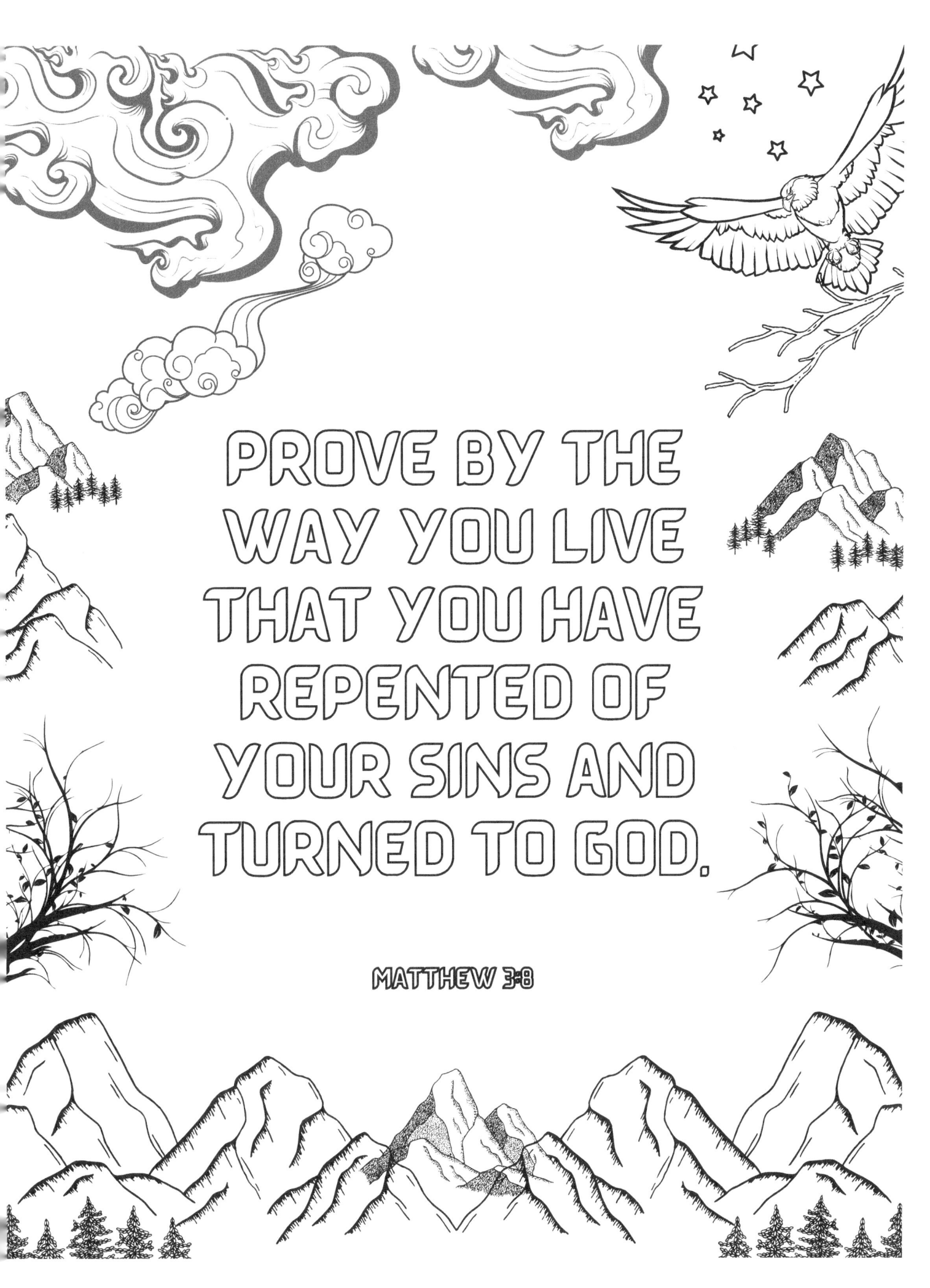

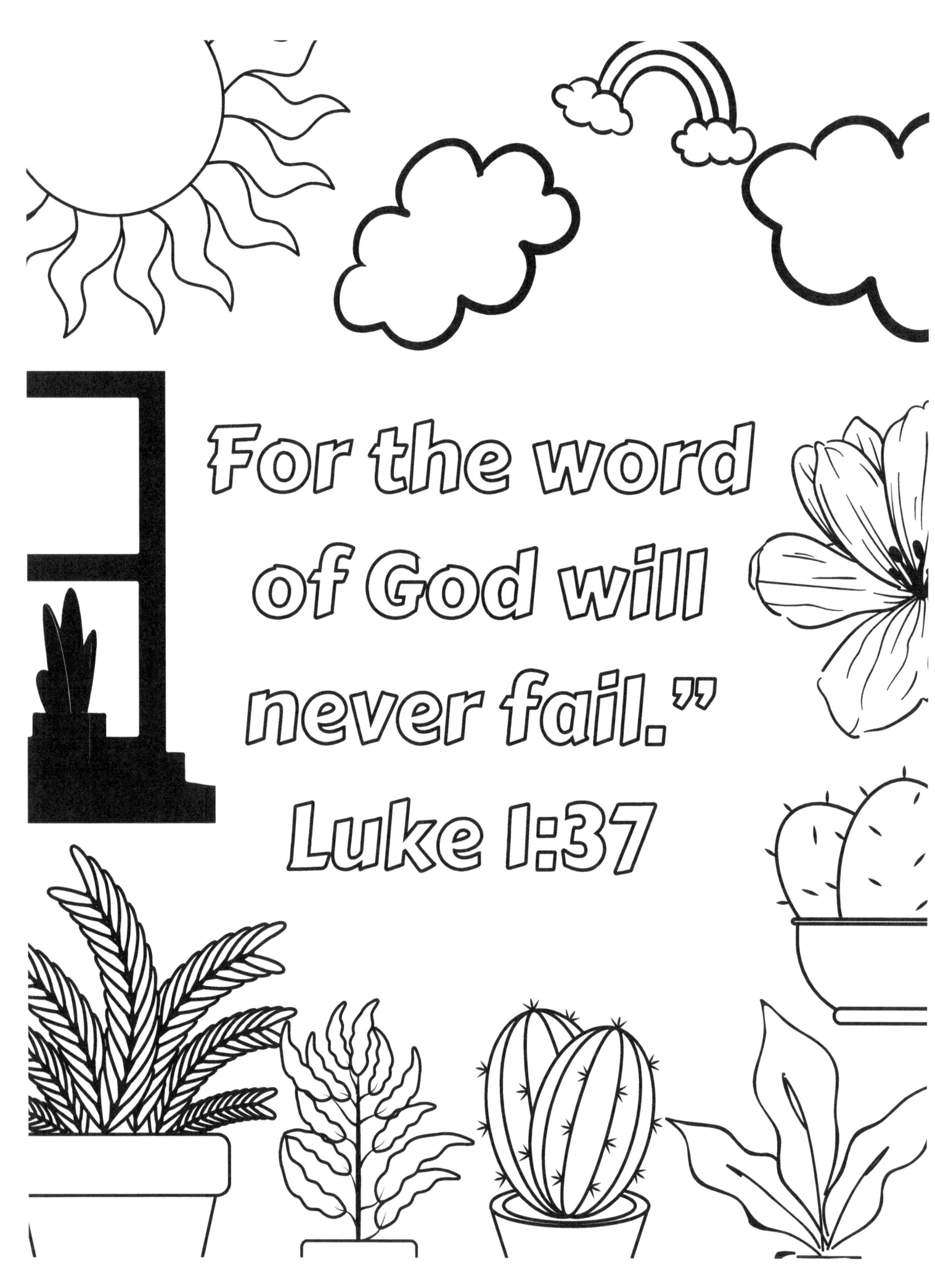

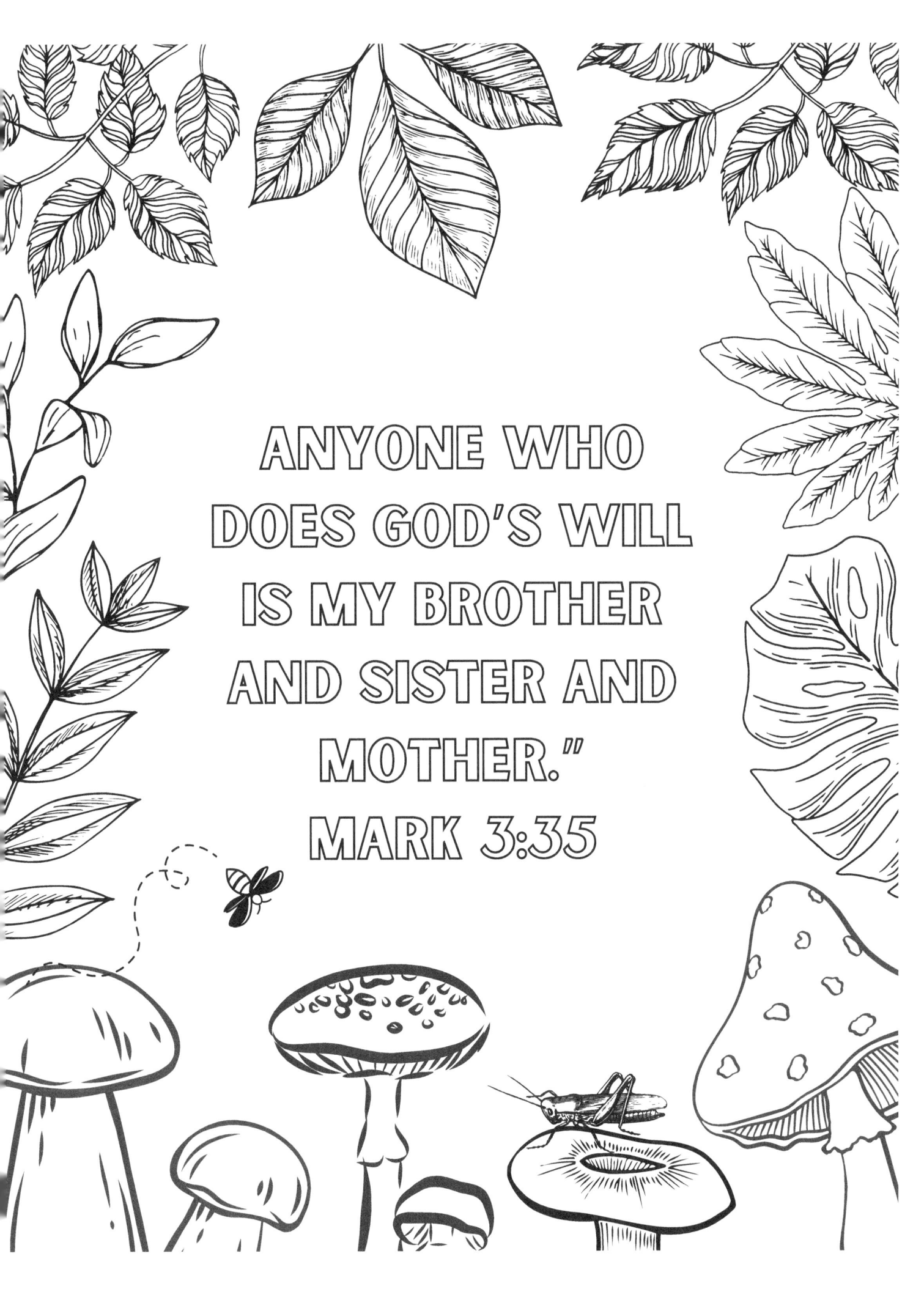

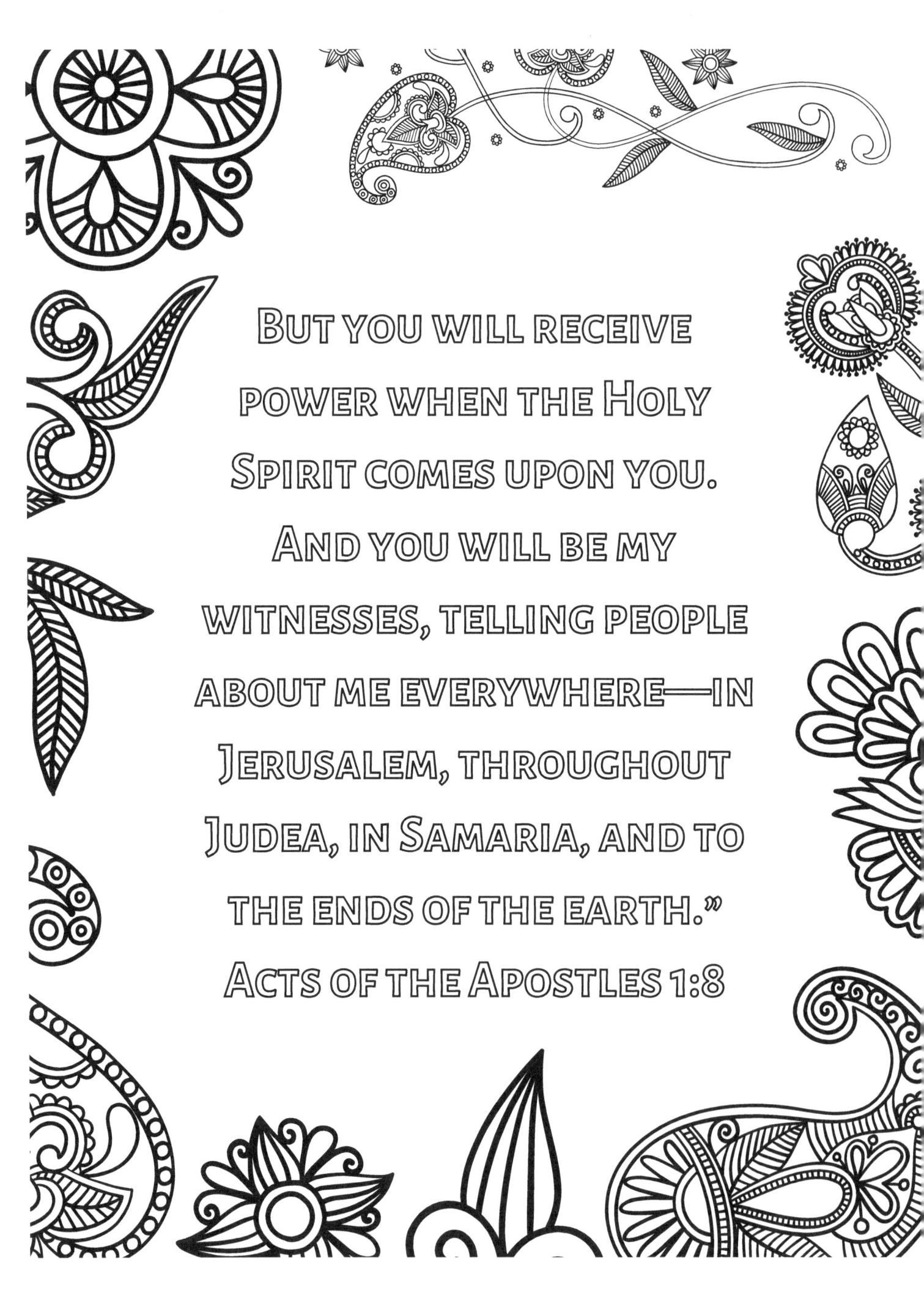

"But you will receive power when the Holy Spirit comes upon you. And you will be my witnesses, telling people about me everywhere—in Jerusalem, throughout Judea, in Samaria, and to the ends of the earth."
Acts of the Apostles 1:8

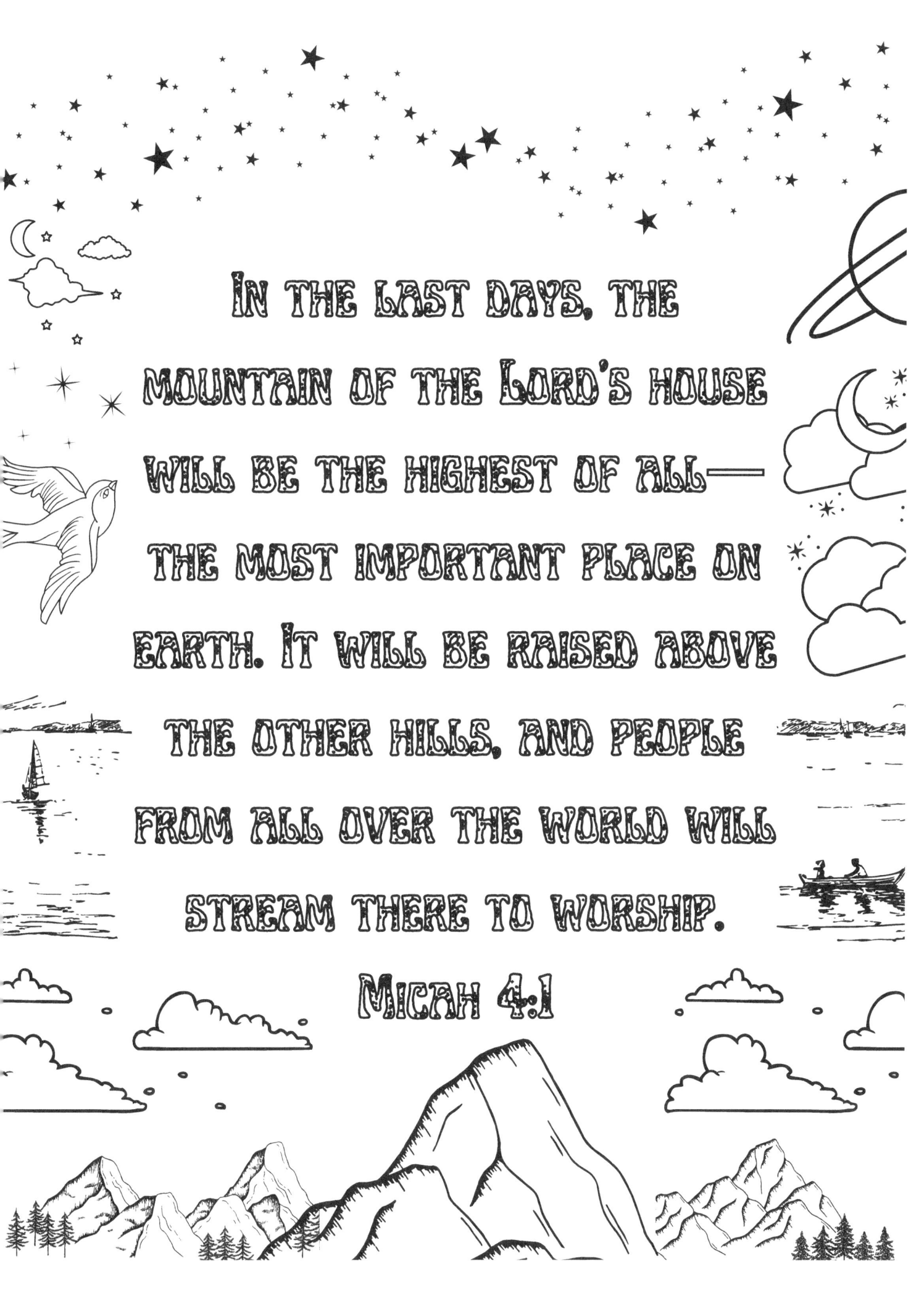

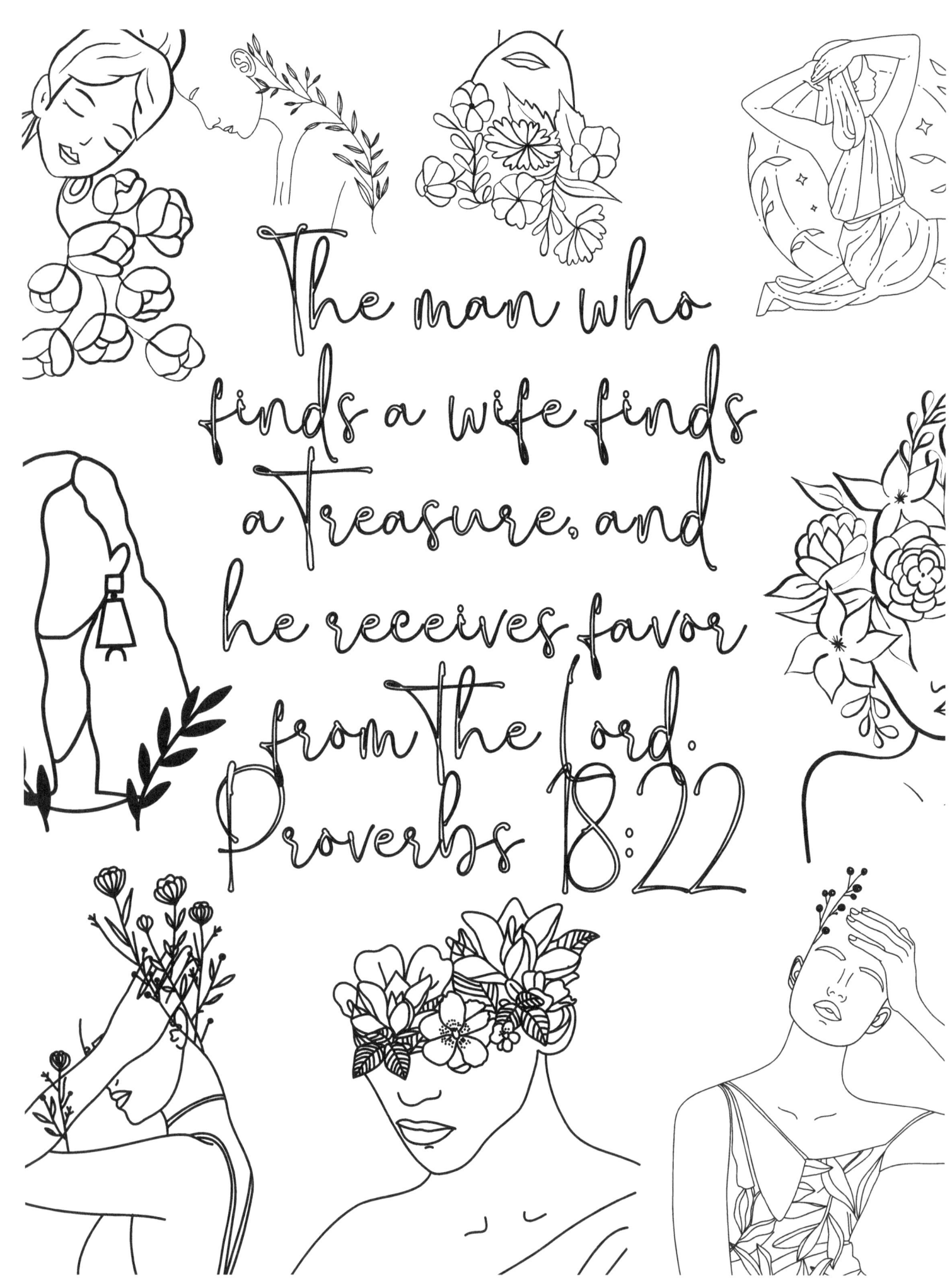

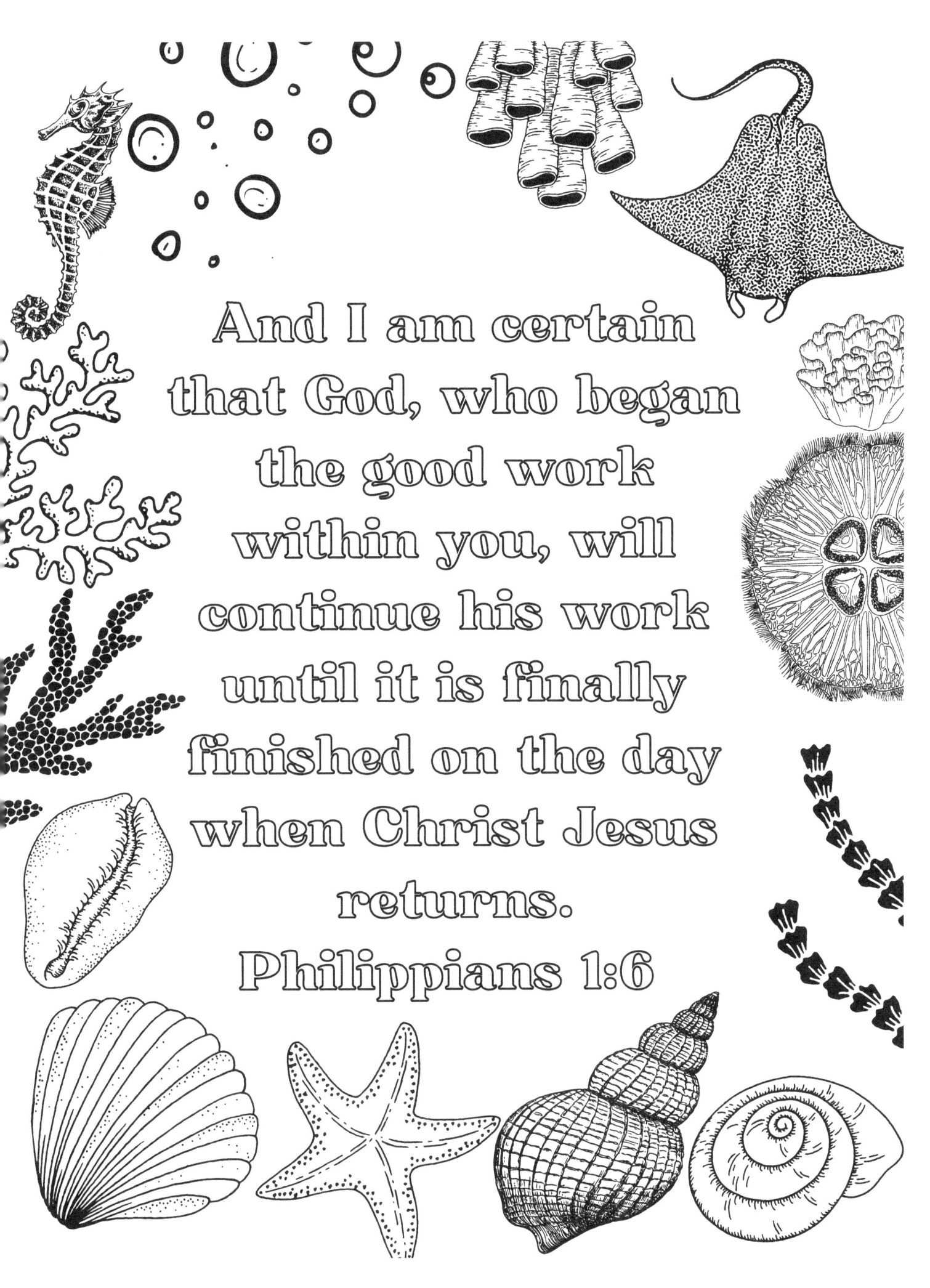

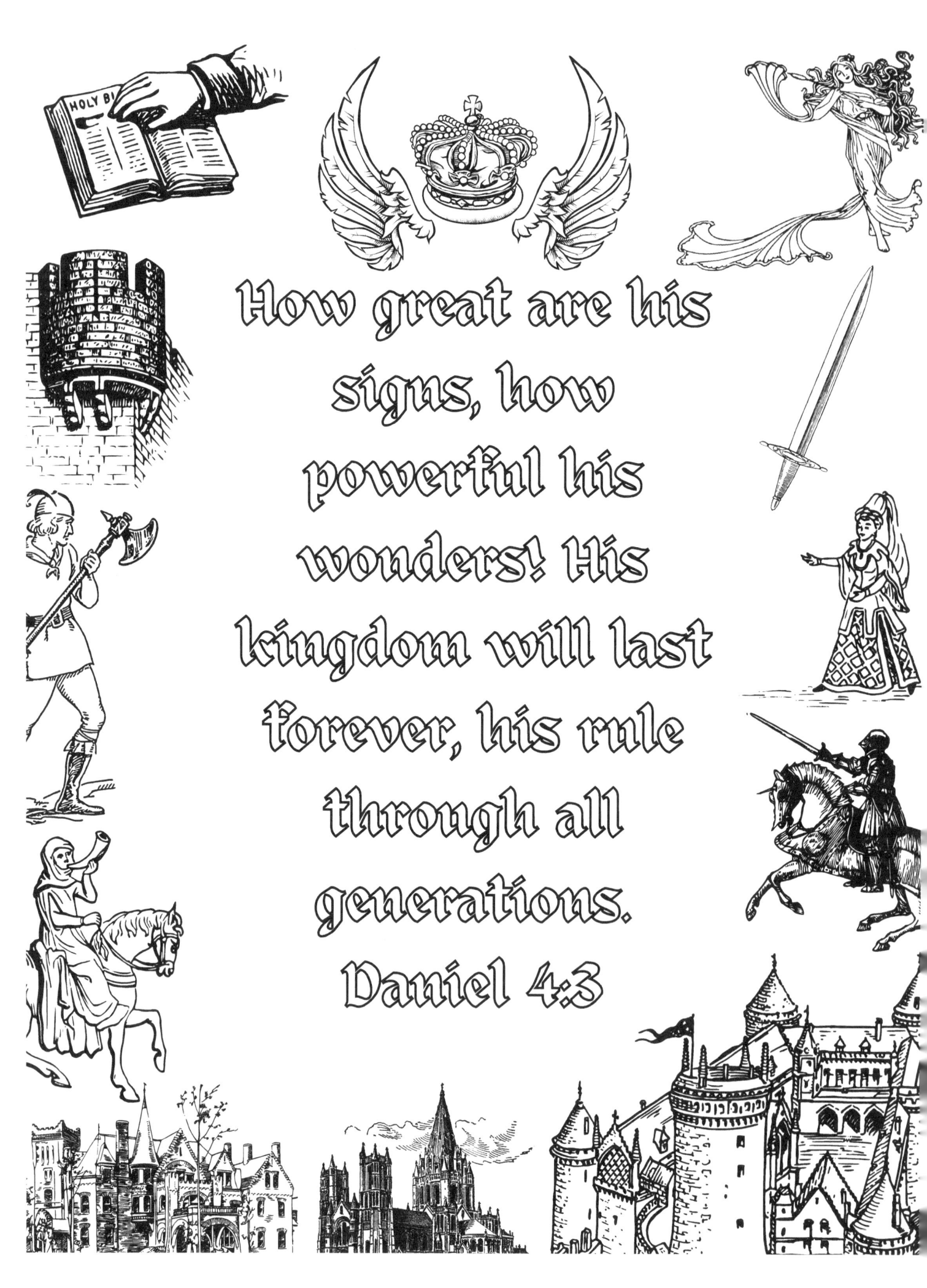

How great are his signs, how powerful his wonders! His kingdom will last forever, his rule through all generations.

Daniel 4:3

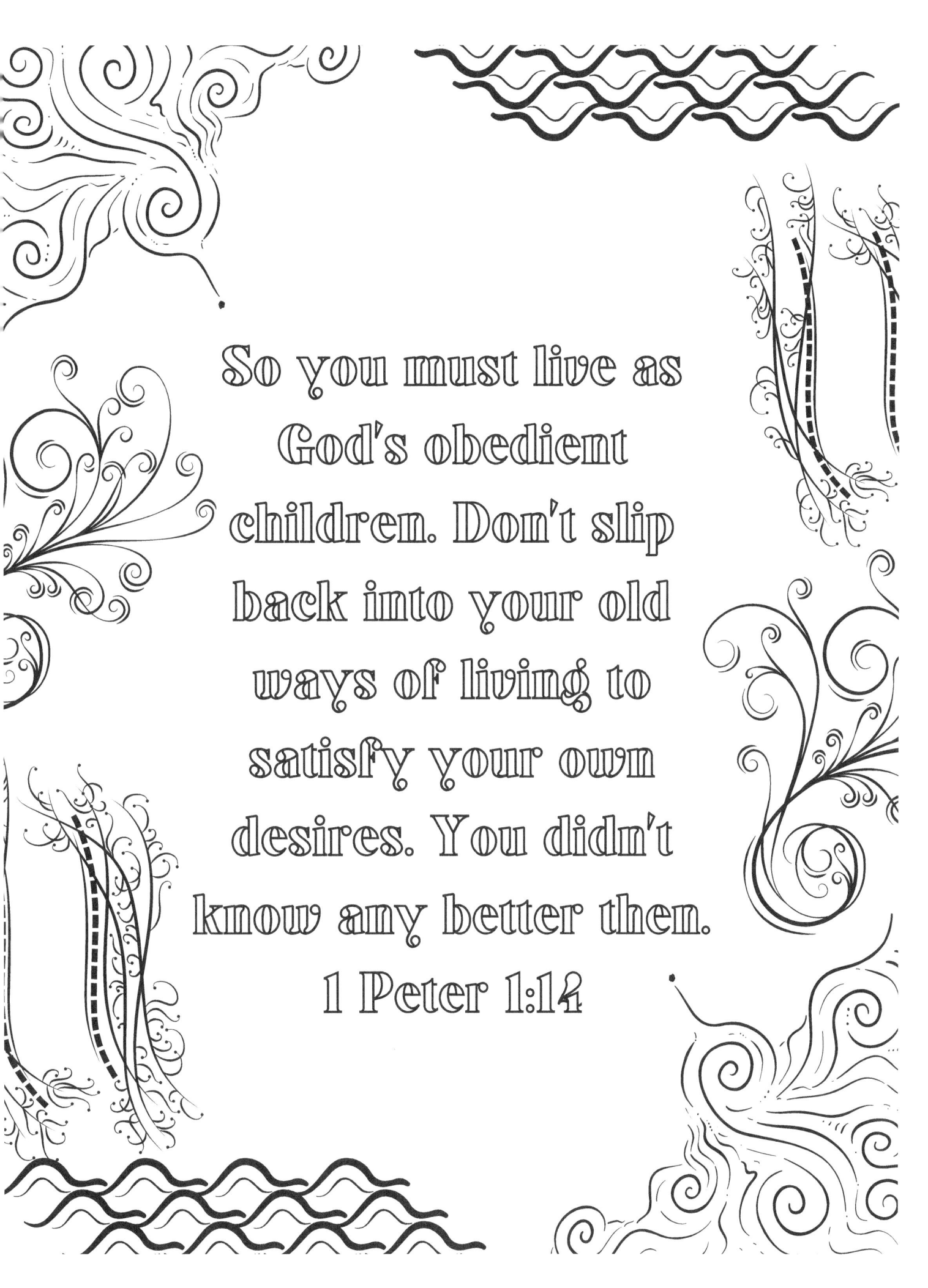

So you must live as God's obedient children. Don't slip back into your old ways of living to satisfy your own desires. You didn't know any better then.
1 Peter 1:14

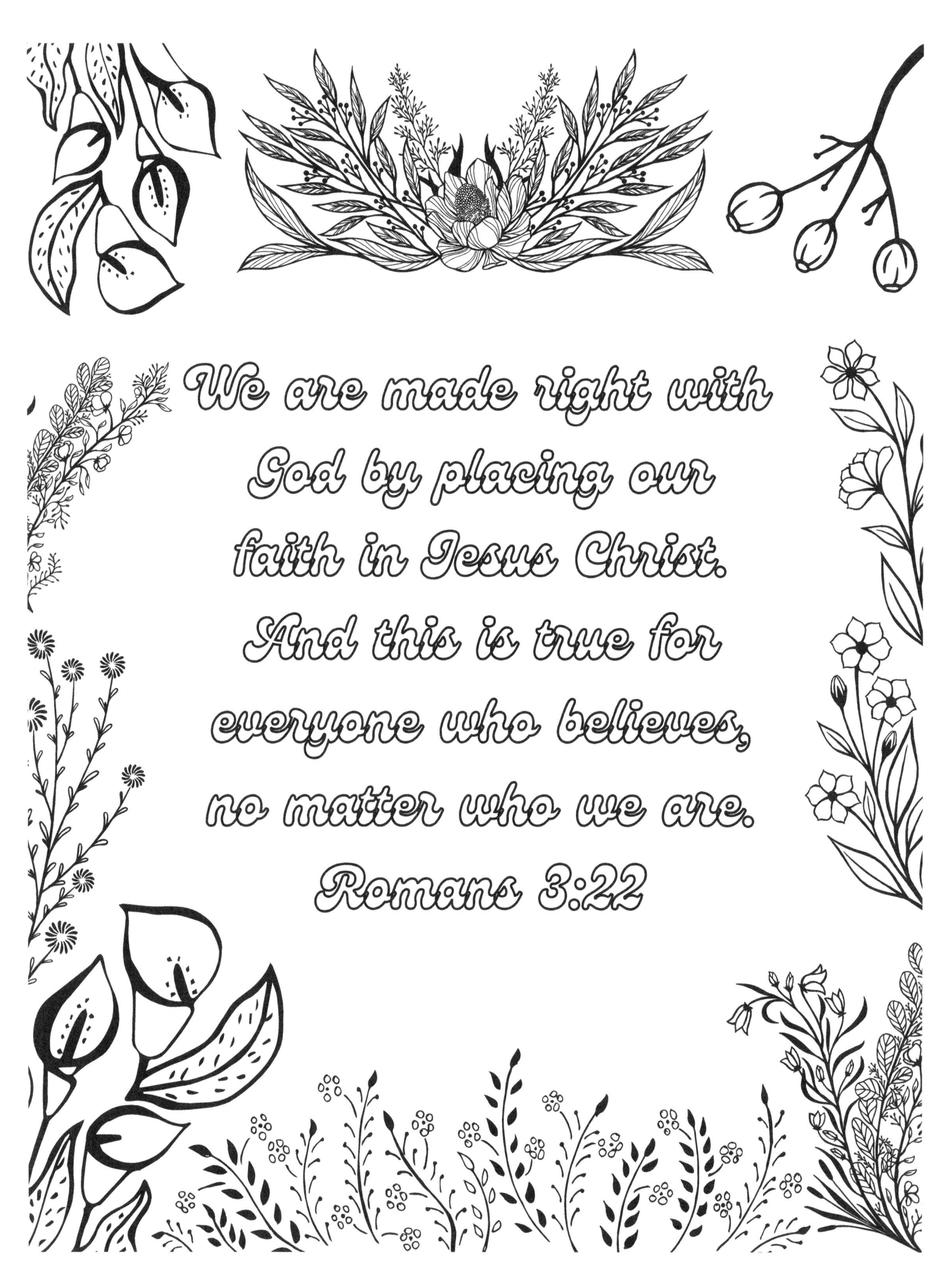

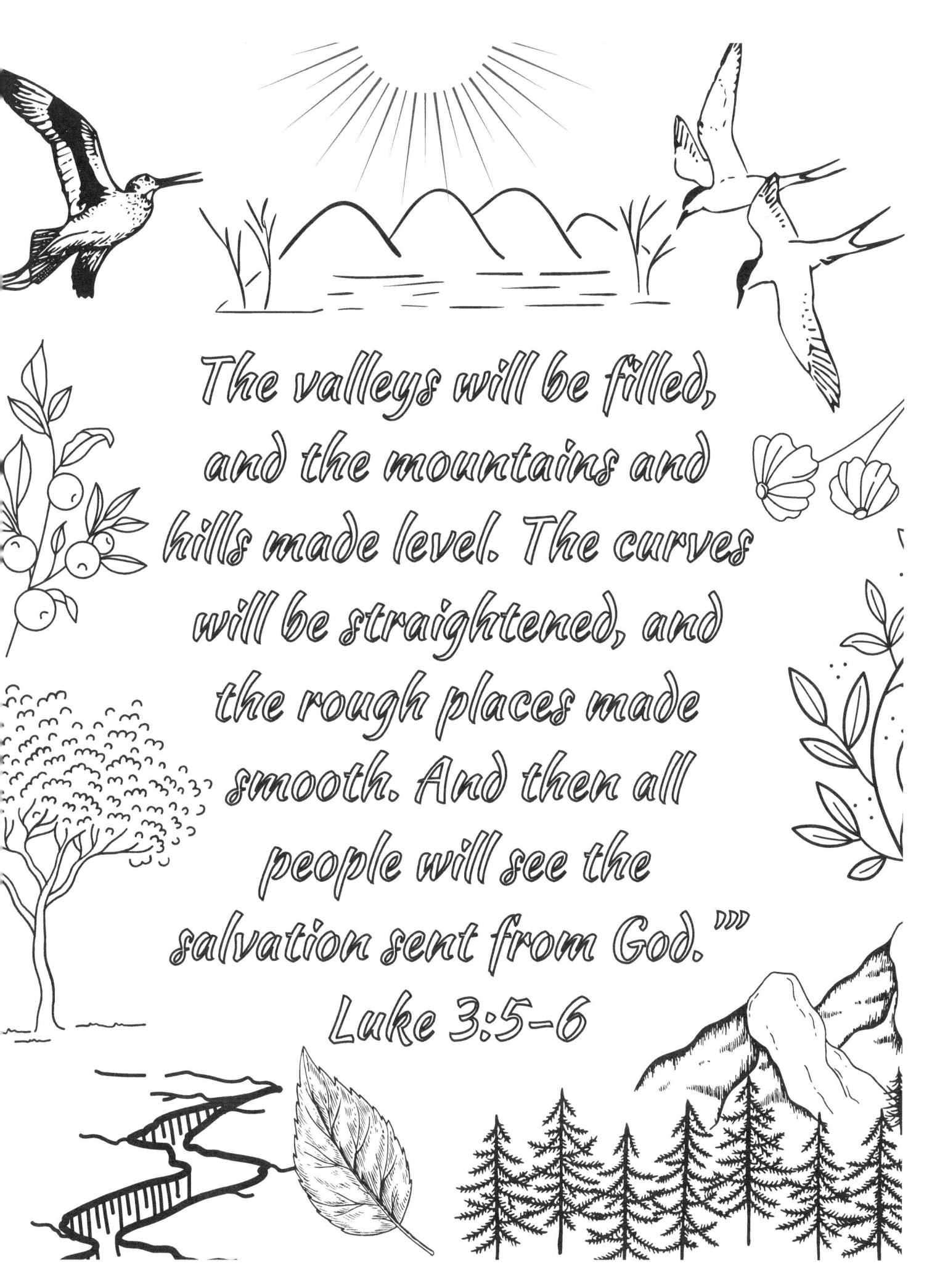

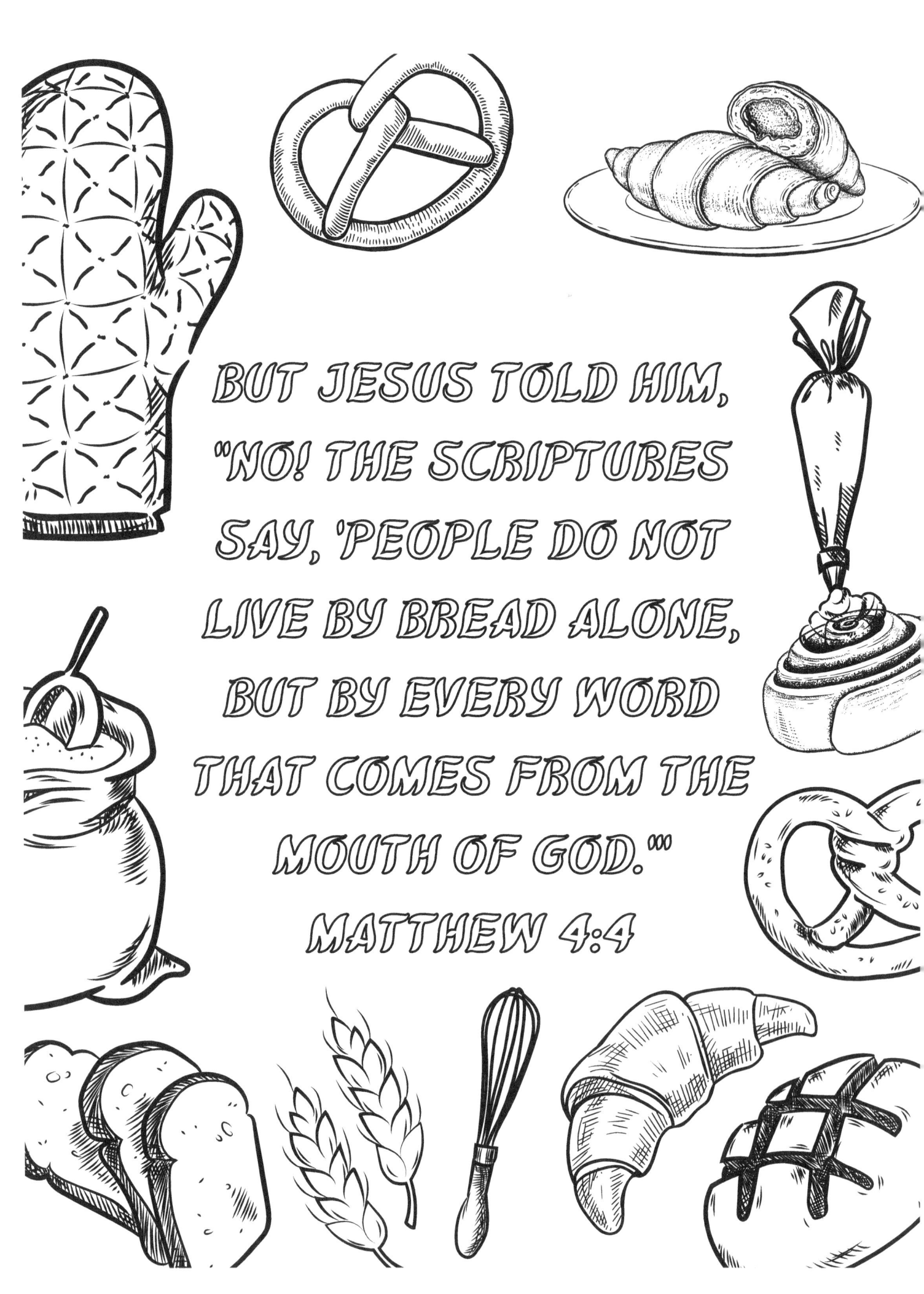

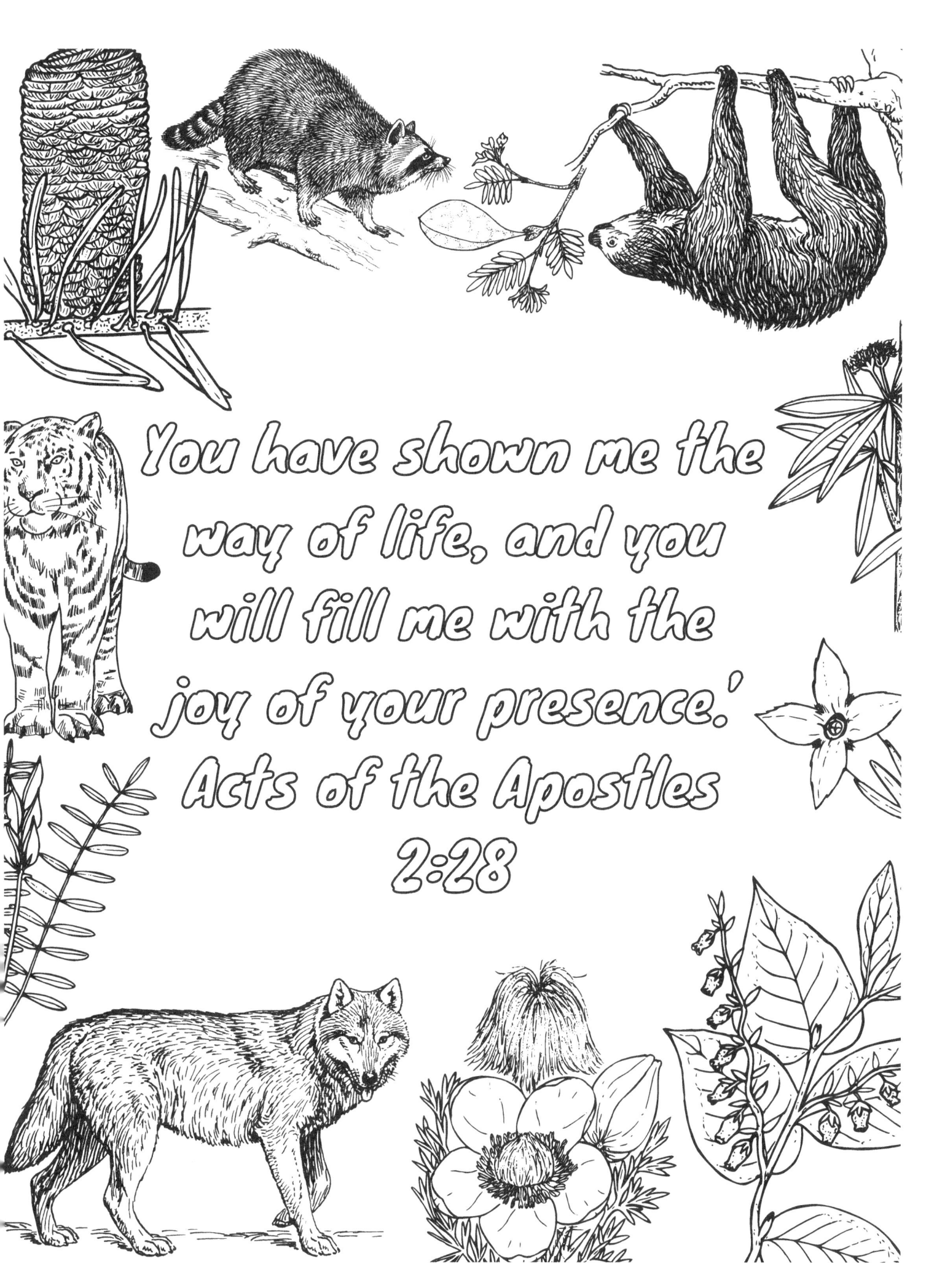

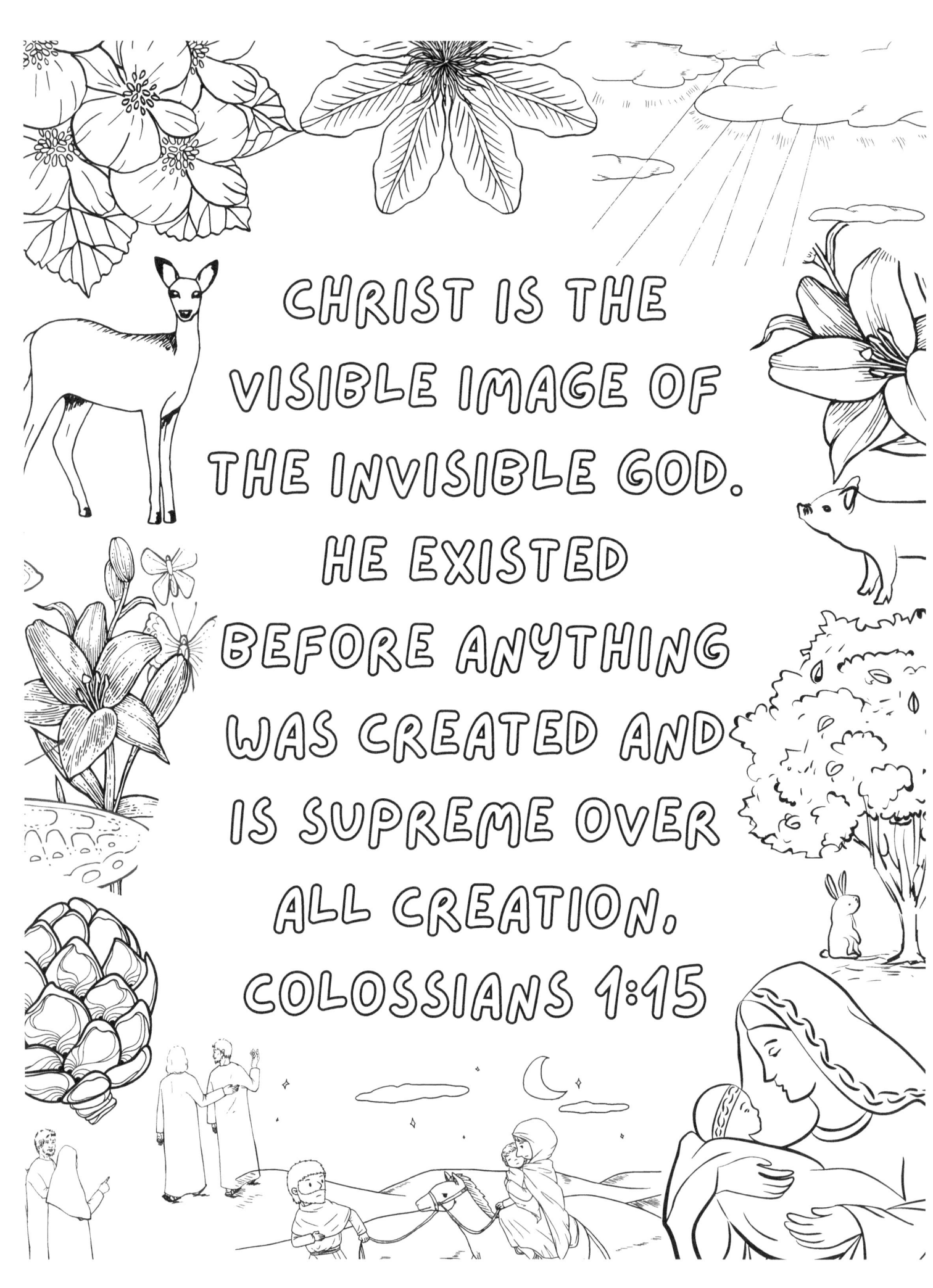

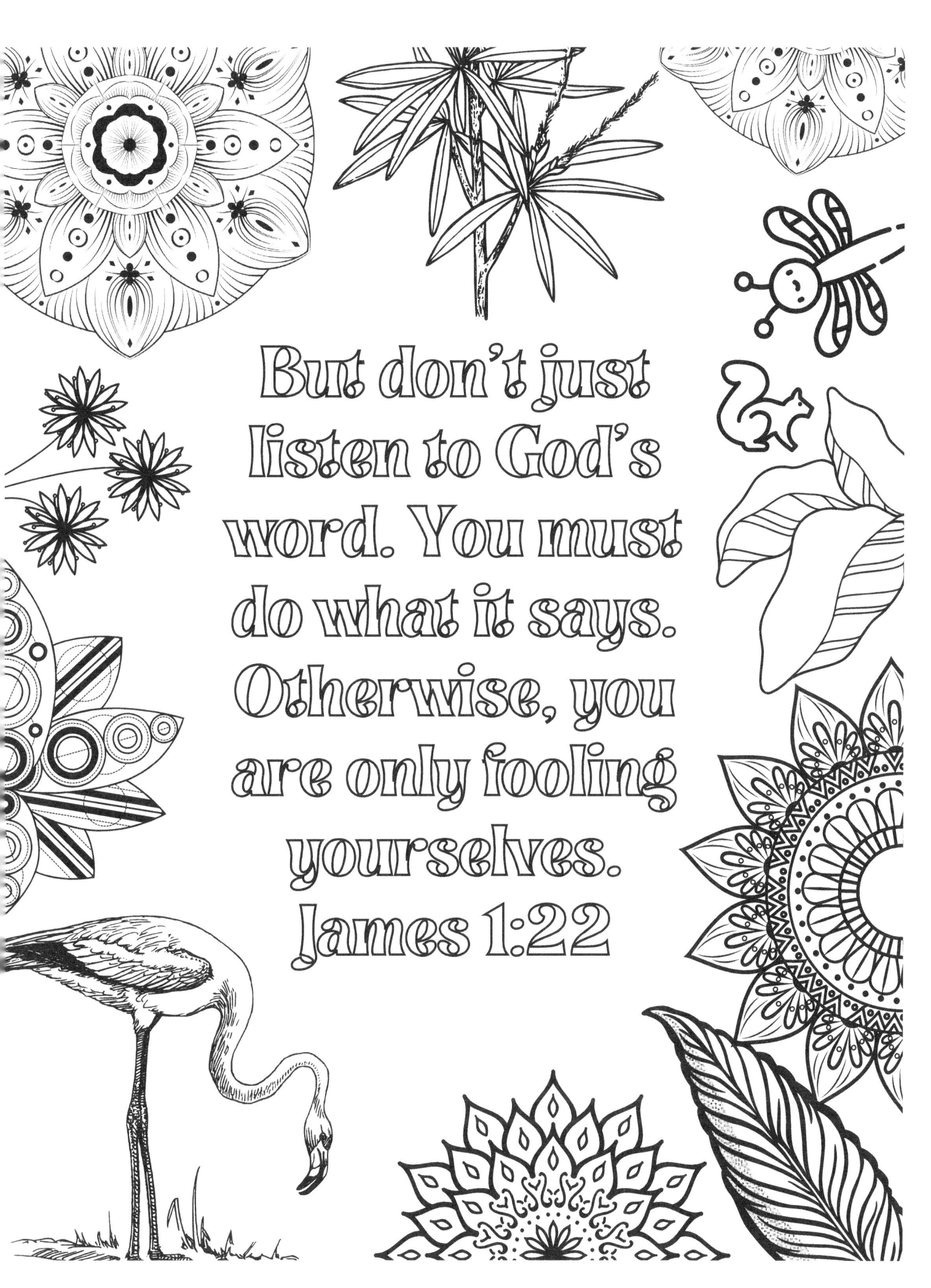

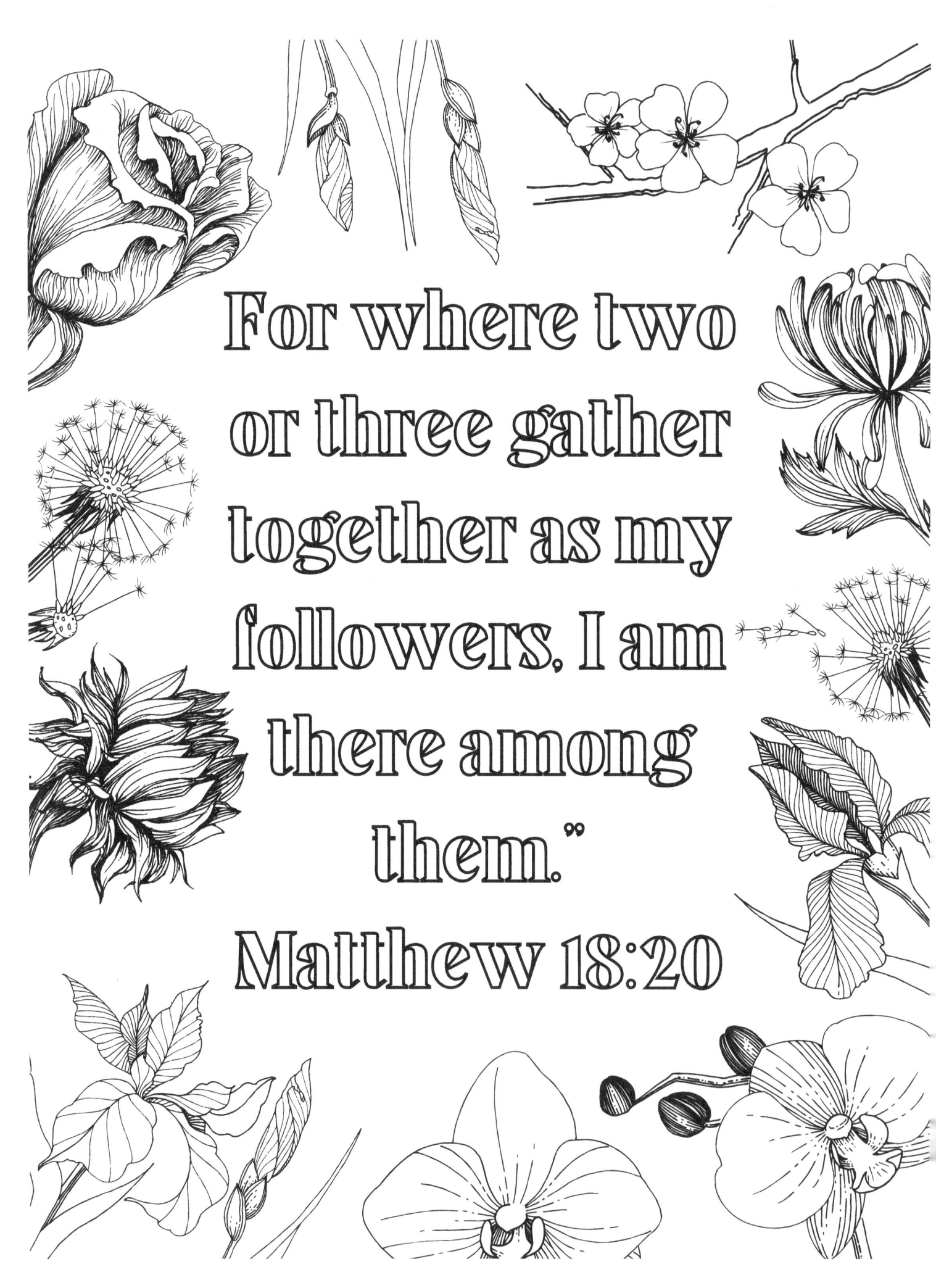

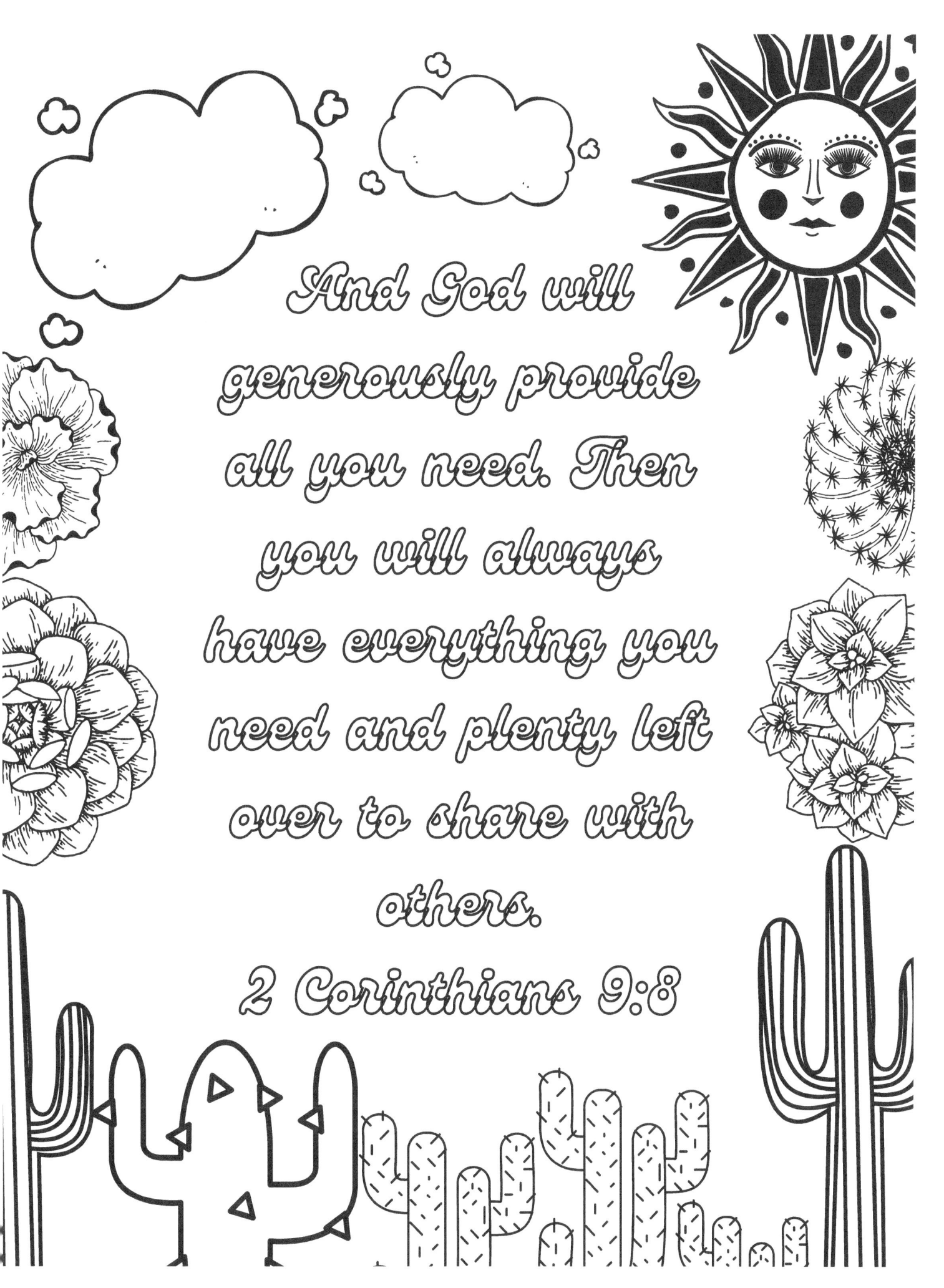

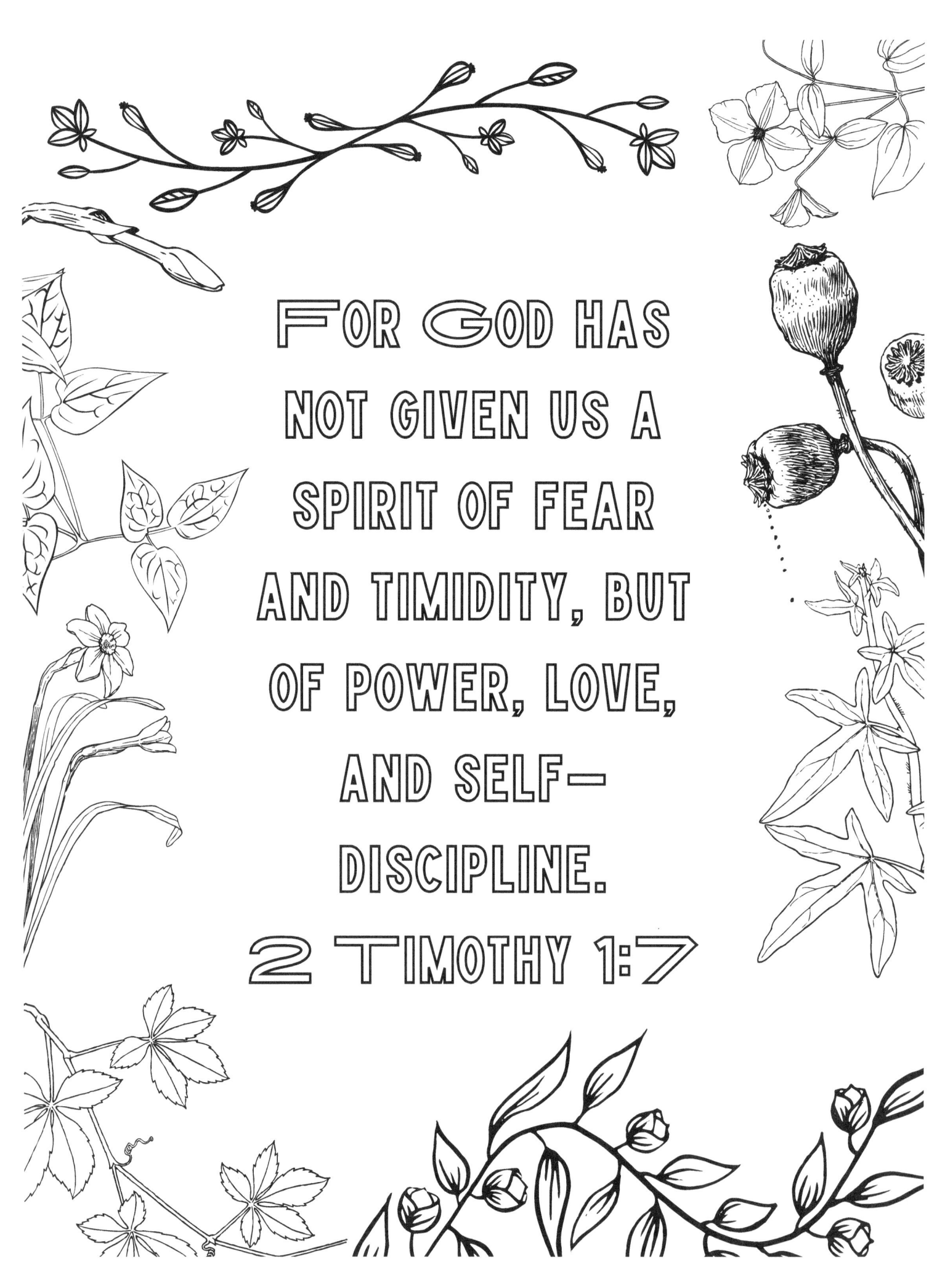

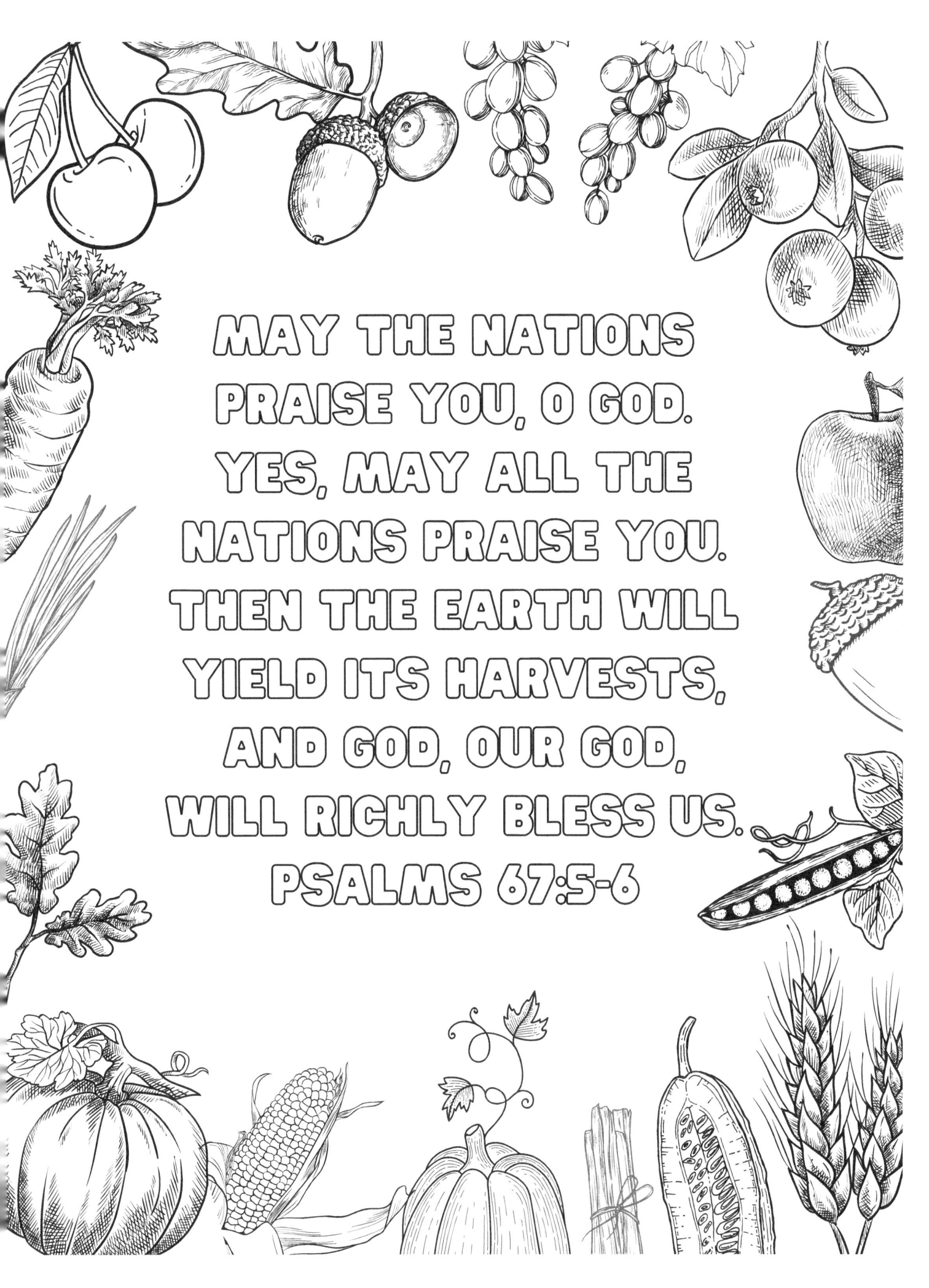

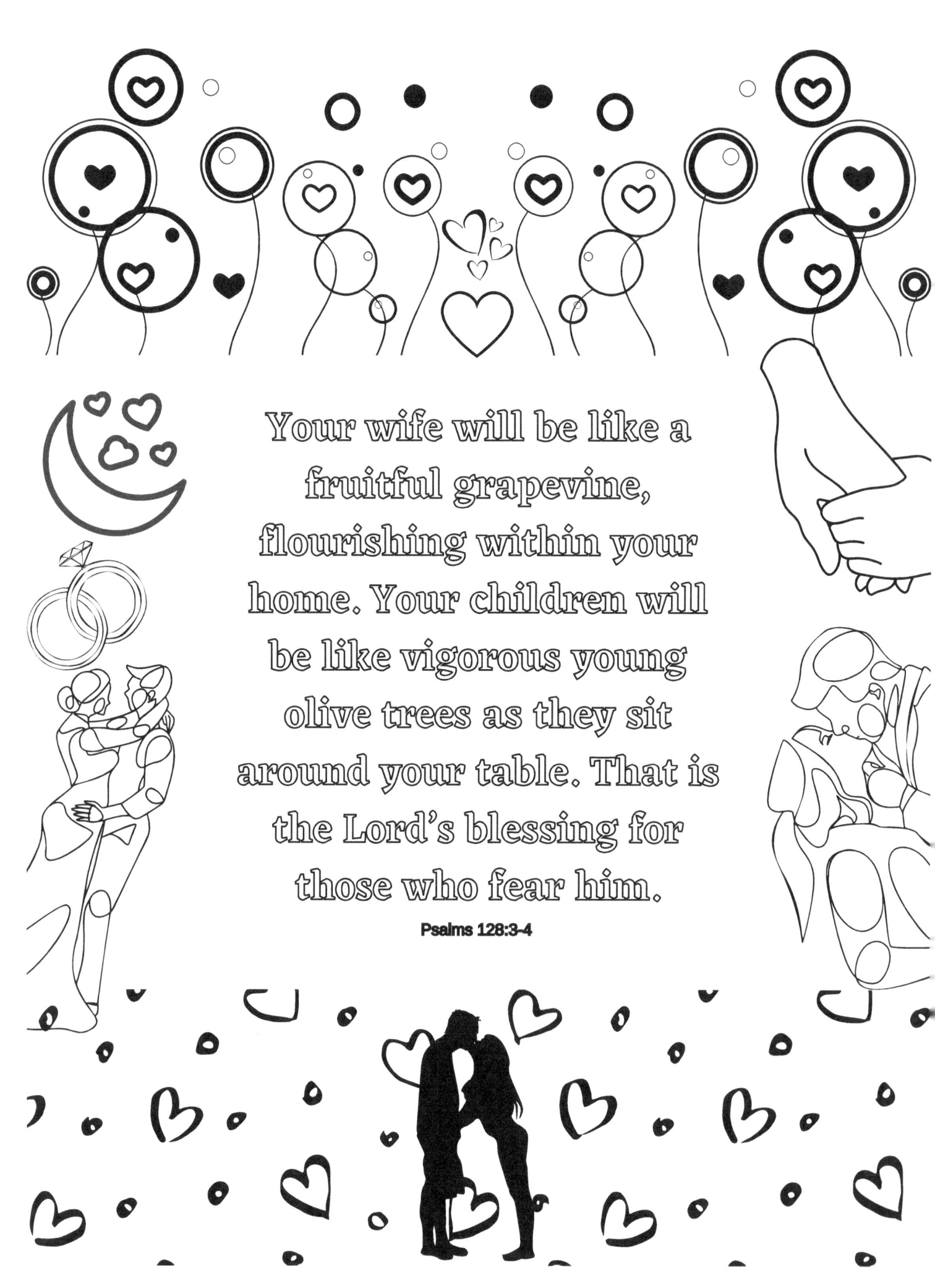

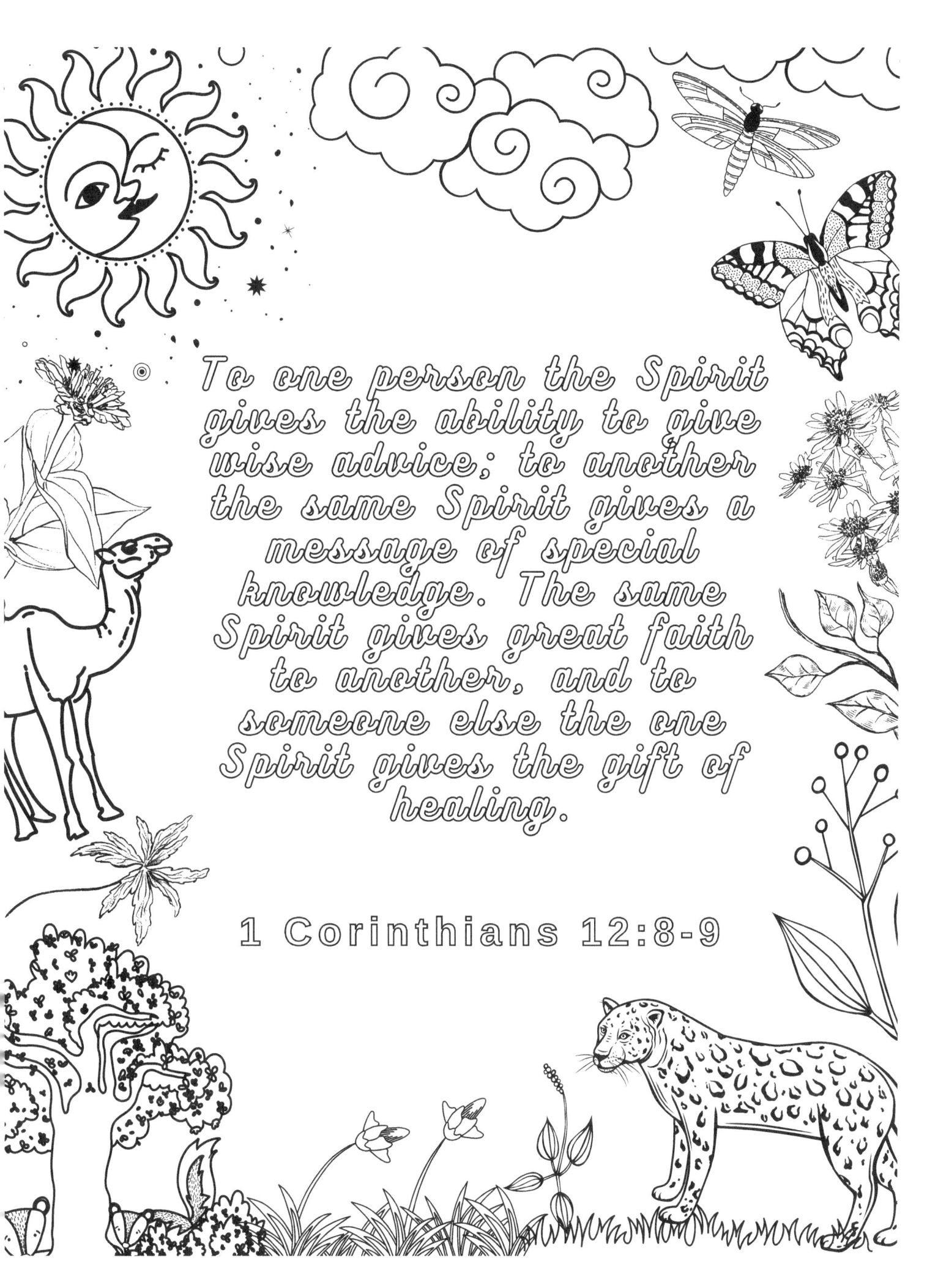

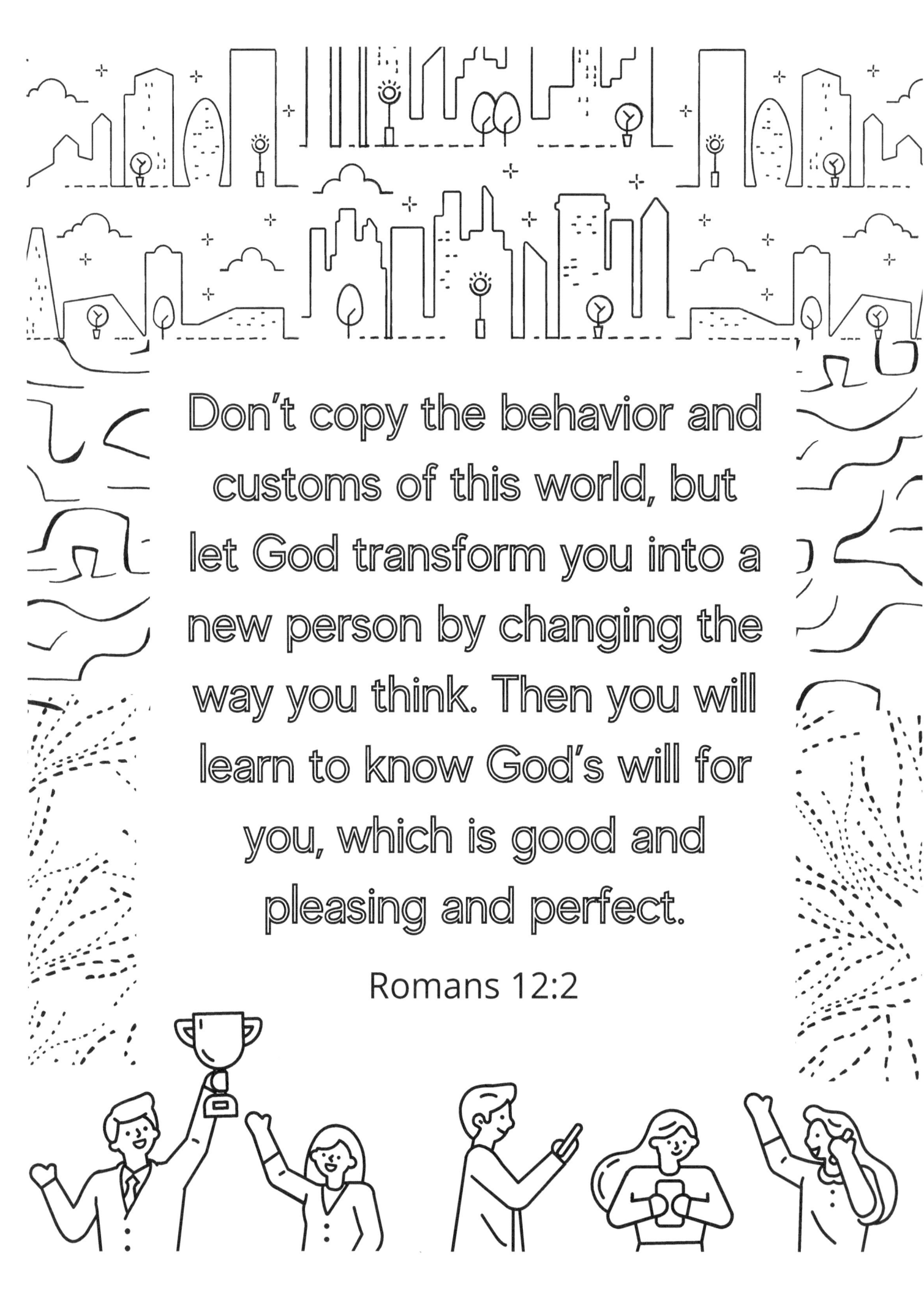

www.ingramcontent.com/pod-product-compliance
Lightning Source LLC
Chambersburg PA
CBHW060006230526
45472CB00008B/1968